China's O

"*If you ever wondered what God could do with a fully surrendered heart, China's Oasis is the book for you. David's story is as grand and fascinating as the country in which it is based.*

From the smallest of beginnings with one child called Rose to a organisation spread all over the world, this is a human story of compassion, love, and generosity. Heartbreaking and hope-filled at one and the same time, David's journey with China's abandoned children is the kind of gritty and courageous inspiration we need for this time.

This book should come with a warning label. Don't read it if you wish to remain sceptical about the kindness of the human heart."

– Andrew Gardener, Senior Pastor, Vine Church, Hong Kong

"*The book you hold in your hands represents the work, sacrifice and love of hundreds of people over the past twenty-five years. Led and inspired by Dave Gotts, they came from around the world to share their passion and compassion with children in China.*

This book is also testament to God's love, exhibited through so many lives in so many ways. As ICC embarks on its second quarter-century of providing love, hope, and opportunity to children with disabilities, we look to the accomplishments of the past while relying on God's guidance for the future."

– Peter Maize, CEO, ICC

"*This is a truly amazing story of an organization dedicated to caring for the 'least of these', told through the lives of those who dared to believe for the impossible.*"

– Tony Read, Chairman, The Justice Conference Asia

"China's Oasis *is a heartbreaking and heart-warming read. The first chapter had me hooked. The authors tell the ICC story honestly as insiders with outsider objectivity, which is no small feat. I ended up with an even greater appreciation for this NGO and the ordinary people who have created such an extraordinary organisation."*

– Gregory Anderson, Senior Pastor, Union Church, Hong Kong

"Some twenty years ago, my wife and I had the honour of connecting with David Gotts and ICC. Back then we were so moved by David's vision and leadership, and now we are celebrating ICC's continued growth and unique place in serving the beautiful people of China. Thank you, David, for your perseverance and faithfulness.

China's Oasis *captures the joy and tears of this incredible journey. Read it, and be challenged and blessed."*

– Scott Harris, Missions Minister, Brentwood Baptist Church, Tennessee

"It's very easy to look at someone else's life in awe of all they have accomplished while rarely understanding the journey that got them there. This book caused me to remember that anything is possible when we listen to the voice of the One who created us. David Gotts did that, and literally thousands of children are alive today because of it. This is an incredibly inspirational read!"

– Cheryl Weber, Host and Senior Executive Producer of *100 Huntley Street*

"What strikes me so strongly in reading about what God has done to reach these children in China is that David Gotts is an ordinary person just like you and me. He does not walk around with a shimmering halo or a robe made of goat's hair; nor does he

have a staff in his right hand or sandals on his feet. He is simply someone who said, 'Yes, send me', and God did the impossible through him.

When I met David in 2012 at my first fundraising concert for ICC, I found him down-to-earth, friendly and energetic, like someone who could have been part of our Bible study group. Getting to see how he constantly submits himself to God through all of life's journeys with much personal sacrifice has been inspirational.

I'm truly honoured and proud to know him and to have been able to contribute to his life-changing work for these precious children in China."

– Ning Kam, award-winning violinist

"This is a story that needs to be told; one of perseverance and faith, of walking and growing through pain; and of God using broken vessels – which we all are in so many ways – to His glory and for the blessing of many. My wife Christine and I deeply honour David Gotts for his commitment to China's orphans and for his determination to stay on course with God's call on his life, despite many personal difficulties and ministry pressures.

It would be impossible to quantify the impact for good that has taken place through ICC's direct and indirect influence in China, and the orphans' lives in particular that have been changed for the better as a result. The issues David and Linda have had to walk through in their own lives only add to the poignancy of that.

We also deeply appreciate that David's obedience and perseverance have paved the way for many others to follow their own China call, not to mention other ministries that have been launched."

– Ross Paterson, Founder, Antioch Missions/Chinese Church Support Ministries, and Director, Derek Prince Ministries China

"I had the great honour of meeting David and Linda Gotts and the ICC team in the spring of 2016. It was an encounter with living saints. These are men and women who have said an unqualified yes to God's intent to restore his beautiful but broken creation.

The story of David's vision for the neglected and abandoned children of China, and his collaborative work with the Chinese government to provide loving care and nurture to these children, is one of the most riveting and inspiring of our age, or indeed any age. Step into these pages, into this story, and see for yourself."

– Mark Buchanan, author, Your Church is Too Safe

"This book provides a poignant window into what life looks like when it's lived for something larger than self; for things God cares deeply about. China's Oasis overflows with aspiration and ache, grit and glow, progress and pain."

– Jedd Medefind, President, Christian Alliance for Orphans

"Some stories need to be recorded and retold, and this is one of them. This tender and compelling biography of David's life not only melted my heart but rekindled in my spirit what inspiration and courage look like. It documents a remarkable life lived with faith and passion in the face of trial and adversity. Simply inspiring!"

– Terence Rolston, President, Focus on the Family Canada

China's Oasis

Love, Hope, and Opportunity

for the Hidden Children of China

David Gotts and Richard Harris

MONARCH
BOOKS

Published by Lion Books
an imprint of
Lion Hudson Limited
Wilkinson House, Jordan Hill Business Park, Banbury Road,
Oxford, OX2 8DR, England
www.lionhudson.com/lion

ISBN 978 0 85721 901 5
e-ISBN 978 0 85721 902 2

First edition 2018

Acknowledgments
Scripture quotations are taken from the *Holy Bible, New International Version*, copyright © 1973, 1978, 1984 International Bible Society. Used by permission of Hodder & Stoughton, a member of the Hodder Headline Group. All rights reserved. 'NIV' is a trademark of International Bible Society. UK trademark number 1448790.

A catalogue record for this book is available from the British Library

Printed and bound in the UK, April 2018, LH26

Contents

Acknowledgments

The authors would like to thank all of the people who have consented to be interviewed and to have their stories told. We would like to thank Chloe Banks for transcribing many interviews into a first draft and Joy Tibbs of Lion Hudson for turning the final draft into a professional production.

This book does not endeavour to tell every tale and cannot mention everyone by name; however, this story and all that has taken place belongs just as much to you as it does to those named in these pages.

We have been as faithful to the story as possible, without softening the impact, because our message is that faith in Jesus, love, and persistence – through adversity – have been the key to our longstanding work in China. We have done our best to be accurate and authentic, so we have not glossed over mistakes made in building ICC because they were opportunities to learn – for us and perhaps for readers too. On occasion, we have distanced individuals from their actions by using assumed names. We have also used assumed names for children to protect those in vulnerable positions. Adults who have given interviews and or remain in ICC's care are named.

This book is dedicated to all those who have been a part of building ICC. We recognize the fortitude of the ICC overseas volunteers through hardship and their selfless giving of themselves, sometimes paying a high personal price. We are even more thankful for the local Chinese staff, who frequently resist the pressures of family, friends, and society to work for the disadvantaged children who make up the ICC family. Together, we carry the privilege and burden day to day, of caring for each precious child. You can follow what ICC is doing today on the website that accompanies this book (www.chinasoasis.com).

We finally honour those who did so much for ICC in roles big and small who have been called home. They belong forever to the ICC family:

Bette Jackson
Dawn Gage
Kieran Gotts
Rex Hills
Rich Hubbard
Terry Phillips.

Foreword

My first encounter with ICC was in the summer of 2007, when my family and I travelled to the Hengyang Welfare Centre to visit the orphanage where our adopted Chinese daughter, Colleen, lived for the first eleven months of her life. I did not have the opportunity to see that facility in 2001 when I came to Hunan to adopt her, as the orphanage workers brought her to my hotel in Changsha.

I learned later of the horrific conditions that existed at that facility before ICC started working there, which led to an 85 per cent mortality rate among the newly abandoned, sick and disabled children and infants. I like to think that Colleen was spared the worst of the conditions as she was a healthy, beautiful baby girl – the kind valued by baby traffickers for their value to American families seeking to adopt. Rather, it was the children with physical disabilities, cerebral palsy, Down's syndrome, and other needs who were discarded into the infamous dying rooms.

In collaboration with a reform-minded Chinese government, ICC began to rescue those children when it came to the Centre in 2004. My family has seen first-hand the positive change ICC's dedicated staff and volunteers have brought the children of China.

I commend this book and ICC to anyone wanting to make a difference with their time or treasure.

Sheila Bair, former Chair of the US Federal Deposit Insurance Corporation (2006–11) during the 2008 financial crisis

At the time we committed to China, we didn't know the cost of this commitment to ourselves or to the organization. We didn't know then that hope would come through suffering and sacrifice.

We didn't know about the lives that would slip through our fingers; we didn't know the tears we would cry, or the fights we would fight – or the children we would not be able to say "yes" to, and that we would feel we had forsaken.

We didn't know the disappointments and inadequacies we would carry. We didn't know if any of this would work, and we didn't know where we would end up. We just hoped in the best way we could.

God has been immensely faithful. The road has been rough but He has been with us all the way. He has transformed the lives of the children, and given them hope and fullness of life. He has done exceedingly abundantly above all we ever hoped for. To Him be the glory, forever.

The journey is not over, there is still much to do, there are still lives to protect and still more glory to be seen. May our hearts remain soft to Him and for China's children now and into the coming years.

Kyla Alexander, ICC China Director
At the opening of the new Heng Yang building in May 2015

CHAPTER 1

Rose

David was facing a big round Chinese gate. It was a large, upright circle with the base buried in the ground to make a pathway. The frame of the circle was faded red and the high walls on either side were rendered in rough concrete.

Originally these moon gates were only found in the gardens of rich Chinese nobles. The irony of that did not escape David's thoughts. Beyond this gate he waited while the doorman opened the iron railings to let them in. Through the bars he had his first glimpse of what he had come to see: a real Chinese orphanage.

David Gotts was twenty-two years old in that January of 1993. The rusty bars made a harsh noise as the gate opened with a jerk. Dirty white buildings surrounded a broken concrete courtyard lined with drains that made perfect runs for huge rats.

The buildings looked dilapidated, but they were relatively new; they just hadn't been maintained. The concrete showed through fallen paint like stains on a tablecloth, and the dark tiles of the roof were patchy. The winter in southwest China was penetratingly cold and usually wet, and the constant humidity pained and permeated everything with a heavy persistent dampness.

There were children in the courtyard but David didn't recognize this fact at first. There was little noise, no laughing and playing, none of the shouting or running that he had expected.

As he moved from the courtyard to the orphanage rooms, he encountered what appeared to be lifeless rag dolls lying in beds or sitting in chairs, with no light in their eyes. They didn't show any emotion, they didn't smile or cry.

"These children had become totally disconnected from the world. The absence of care and love had caused their eyes to grow dim as they gave up on expecting to receive love. I had never seen anything like it."

David's friend Chan Kit Ying had been working as a volunteer in the orphanage for six months. She guided him through the building, down a corridor into the first room, a baby room. It was a reasonable size, but despite that it was full to bursting with rows of dark green wooden cribs.

David peered into the first one, not too sure what he expected to see. Although Kit Ying and some other friends had shared a little of the realities of the situation in Chinese orphanages, this was the first time that he would see it for himself.

Inside the crib was not one, but five babies. Some were wriggling, some still, their legs and arms constrained from moving by the confusing mass of pink and grey padded winter clothes. David carefully unwrapped the layers of clothes of one baby to check the condition of the child within. He recoiled from the sight of scabies and painful weals covering the baby's body. None of the babies had proper cloth nappies[1] but each wore an old rag, or plastic milk powder bags tied loosely around the waist with rough cord. As he picked up a baby, the plastic milk bag diaper fell away revealing bedsores and nappy rash. David felt a physical ache that ran right through him.

It was then that the smell hit him. The smell of soiled cloth, combined with sour milk, a damp rotting smell mixed with urine. It was the pervasive smell of institutionalized babies and toddlers.

There was something more hanging in the air. The charcoal

briquette heater that was used to heat the room gave off an acrid smell that burned at the back of his throat. The ramshackle chimney struggled to vent the highly toxic smoke. If the chimney were to become blocked the carbon monoxide would rapidly remove the last vestiges of life from the motionless babies crammed into every cot. The smoke, combined with sour milk and wet nappies, remained David's identifying smell of every orphanage he was to visit from then on.

The babies made no noise. New intakes might cry, but even as newborns they soon learned that crying did not lead to attention. They were cried out. Exhausted. David was shocked. He watched as a government worker came into the room with a tray full of baby bottles. She distributed them quickly, putting a bottle on a pillow by each baby's head in preparation for a technique known as prop-feeding.

Each baby then began a desperate search for the teat of the bottle, but more often knocked the bottle so that it rolled out of reach. After a short time, the government orphanage caregiver would sweep up the bottles, some barely touched.

Seeing each baby starved of food and human contact David was numb; overwhelmed. "I could pick up one bottle and help one baby, but what of the forty or fifty others?" And so many seemed already to have given up; their eyes blank and lifeless. He tried to make eye contact but the babies he peered at just stared into the distance.

David wasn't the only one overwhelmed. The sheer numbers of babies overwhelmed the few staff employed to provide care. Their faces and hearts had necessarily hardened, for they knew that even with the most gruelling work they could not stem the flood of children nor provide the care that they needed.

In the next room toddlers and small children were placed in little potty chairs made from wood or metal that looked like a kindergarten chair with a hole in the seat. An actual potty or basin would be placed under the hole. On the occasional day when the children were taken outside, the potty chairs were placed over an open drain for the waste to drip through.

In order to make it easier for the few caregivers they reduced the children's mobility, by tying the toddlers' wrists and feet to the chair with plastic twine or scratchy cord. Even if they had wanted to they couldn't move.

David was devastated. "I wanted to untie them all but knew that this would cross a line with the government workers and cause problems for Kit Ying. All I could do was hide my emotions and stroke the cheeks of the little ones. Most of them didn't respond, but one or two felt my touch and leaned toward me to feel the warmth of human contact."

David left this room more shocked than before. Naïve to these wretched realities just a few minutes earlier, it was almost impossible to take in what he was seeing.

Through the courtyard, David came face to face with malnourished pre-teen children with disabilities. Few babies were strong enough to survive but some parents would care for their disabled children for some years until, in the face of stigma and pressure, they would abandon them when the burden became too much.

David knelt in front of one boy but when their eyes met, he was unresponsive; there was no flicker of life. He tried to make others smile, but they looked crushed. The light had gone out of their eyes, and they had given up the will to live.

Moving around the courtyard to the next room he encountered another disturbing sight. The door to this room was locked. Unable to enter, David looked through the barred windows into the room.

Through the haze of smoke he saw a room of children on the verge of puberty, naked from the waist down despite the cold. They were climbing over the furniture like animals in the zoo; he felt that he was looking at a lost humanity. When he asked why they were locked in the room, the government worker casually replied, "*Tamen shen jing bing*" – "They are crazy."

Kit Ying noticed David's expression and asked him if he wanted to continue. He breathed hard – "I think so" – though he wasn't sure that he did.

"There's just one more room," she said.

They climbed the concrete stairs to the second floor, where they pushed open the unlocked door. The room was about three metres square, painted dark green on the lower half of the walls, and white at the top. The paint was faded and chipped so as to make the line between green and white indistinct.

Like most of the rooms, it was dark and gloomy, with a bare cement floor. Inside was a wooden bed frame – a wooden pallet with a thin cotton mattress on top. From the doorway, David could see three babies lying on the mattress.

"It was like someone had taken three rag dolls and tossed them onto a bed. Their bodies lay in unnatural positions. I felt panic well up inside."

As he approached, he looked down, and with deep shock David realized that two of these little girls were dead. It was the first time he had seen a dead human being, and he never forgot the image of their tiny, emaciated bodies. The third baby looked as though she would pass within the hour.

"I felt so helpless and angry at what I was seeing. My whole life, I had seen babies loved, nurtured, given the best that their parents could give. Babies were seen in beautiful nurseries, with smiles, cribs, bedding, and pushchairs. Not here, in this living hell. Death was in that room; death stalked the rooms of that welfare centre; death chose its prey. Death stole the lives of babies that should have known love and care and hope for the future and a life to live. I was gutted."

This was where children from the downstairs baby room were taken to die. When the unending flow of abandoned children filled every crib to overflowing, the overworked caregivers were left with little choice. They would pluck the weakest and most disabled from their cots and take them on a final journey to this room. The babies would be given no more milk and would quickly deteriorate, dying in their own waste, in the soiled rags that they wore.

The caregivers might enlist an older child to inform them when the babies had died. The little bodies would then be put in a rice bag, or not at all, and put out with the trash. The little room that David had entered was just one of many that would become known as the "Dying Rooms".

At that time, most Chinese welfare centres had such rooms. "What I saw as barbaric was the result of years of overwhelming abandonment that challenged many developing countries. When babies are abandoned daily, or more than once a day, the staff become so overwhelmed that the unthinkable becomes normal."

Later that evening, David sat down to process the day with Kit Ying, and began to learn the reality of the situation. After his experience, he felt shocked and indignant, looking for someone to hold responsible. The caregivers, the parents, the decision-makers. "I told Kit Ying that I really couldn't understand how the welfare centre could do this." But as he learned more of the context of the welfare system, he was soon exhausted by trying to pinpoint the blame for a deeply complicated situation.

David tried to take in what Kit Ying was telling him. How welfare centres across China were trying to do the best they could but had very few resources. Staff, who had been given virtually no training, were totally overwhelmed by the daily influx of babies and children, many of them with medical conditions or disabilities. There were just not enough hands to clean beds or feed babies. In China at the time, children were at the bottom of the welfare system pecking order. The elderly were at the top because of the concept of filial piety – and they could make their case loudly.

Kit Ying shared that caregivers in the welfare centre had been assigned their job – it wasn't a choice or vocation. "It is a secure job with a basic income and pension but one that carries a negative social stigma. Each one of them knows there is very little chance for promotion at work and their family looks down at them at home. Their hours are long; they work six days a week, and they each have thirty babies to look after." It helped explain to David why the conditions were so poor.

He understood then that his belief that every human life was precious and of value was an alien concept in China. The nation had experienced centuries of war and disruption followed by a population explosion because of the general improvement in health and security across the country after the Communist takeover in 1949. This had led to the introduction in 1980 of the one-child policy, which caused many unintended consequences. The Communist philosophy that the individual was subservient to society, combined with the state taking responsibility for welfare, had given rise to abandonment on a scale that no country before had ever experienced.

"Why doesn't the government try to stop abandonment?"

"They do. It's illegal!" Kit Ying replied.

David thought back to the family-planning posters that he had seen around the city, which even back in the early 1990s would show a mother, father, and baby girl – never a baby boy. Even then the government was trying to strengthen the value of baby girls. However, it was fighting deep cultural beliefs. Despite the government genuinely wanting to stop abandonment it was clear that both society and government found it easy to allow babies to just disappear.

Kit Ying continued, "But if a couple is faced with the birth of a disabled child, the baby's grandparents may persuade the father to abandon the baby before the mother recovers from childbirth. Children are often abandoned near public offices and police stations so that they can be found before they die in the cold."

They talked late into the night while David explored the cultural and social environment. Rural people for instance didn't want to have a baby girl, as it was just another mouth to feed. China's population had exploded because rural families were used to a high mortality rate and would keep having children until they had enough boys to work the land and take over the farm. Too many extra births led to a tidal wave of abandonment. "Nobody foresaw the impact of girls and disabled children dumped on a welfare system that could not cope."

Meeting Rose

After a restless night, they rose early to go back to the welfare centre. Shortly after their arrival, a caregiver told Kit Ying that another abandoned baby had just arrived. She was just a few hours old. Left naked in a cold winter street, she had been found by a passer-by and taken to the local police station; the police then bundled her off to the welfare centre.

The baby girl lay in a cot in the babies' room. "I'll never forget the moment that I looked into the face of that little baby girl. She was so beautiful… so perfect in every way. I remember thinking that she had no idea what was surrounding her. She didn't know that her parents had abandoned her, or that she was surrounded by suffering and death. She had not yet learned that her cry would raise no response from those responsible to care for her."

David picked up this little bundle. She was so light, like a small bag of sugar, and she was beautiful, with a perfectly formed nose. David observed her bluish eyelids and lips, thinking that she must be cold from having been abandoned in the early hours. Her tiny fingers were wrinkled and her nails grew over the tips of her tiny blue fingers. He had an instant connection. David thought, "This is one child in need and this is happening to me right now. What am I going to do?"

As he looked into the face of this newly abandoned little girl he was struck by what her future would be if she was just left there. With a choke of emotion he realized that if he put her down she would die. This baby's future held nothing but a slow death. He had no idea what to do. What did he think he could do? Would anything he did make any difference? He felt desperate. He turned to Kit Ying and pleaded, "Can we do something?"

David and Kit Ying walked over to the office of the director of the centre and asked permission to take the baby girl out of the babies' room overnight to her apartment nearby. It was granted with a lazy wave. For him, the little girl was just another nameless child. They bundled the baby up and carried her to Kit Ying's apartment nearby. Sitting in the cold room, waiting for the one-bar electric heater to warm the room, he looked down into the face of the baby.

As he gazed at her face, he felt that she was called Rose. It came from… he knew not where. It conjured up a passion in David to change his life, his plan, and his direction – everything.

Rose's tiny lips were still blue after being abandoned in the cold. They warmed her with blankets, taking turns to hold her. As the evening wore on, David returned to his room. Kit Ying spent the night holding the baby close, cuddling her up to her own body warmth. By morning, Rose was coughing up blood.

They sought the director's permission to take her to the local hospital, bundling her into layers of clothing. As they burst out of the welfare centre compound, they hailed a passing *san lun che*, a tricycle taxi supporting a big open engine and a chimney belching a black plume of barely digested diesel. The passengers crammed into the back. It was not far to the hospital and Rose was quickly admitted.

"I walked away from the hospital having left Rose and feeling that I had done something good. This little girl now had a chance with hospital medical care, and better nutrition. There was now a flicker of hope that Rose had a future. So we headed back to the welfare centre."

David and Kit Ying had other babies to care for and other needs to meet. At the end of the day, David wanted to check on little Rose so they jumped in a taxi back to the hospital. They climbed the stairs and walked through the large entrance to the reception area.

"I remember vividly going up to the desk to speak to the records clerk. They turned casually and, as if giving us a weather report, said she was dead."

There are occasions in life when time seems to stop; when the constant din of the road outside fades to silence. "The shouts of the workmen throwing bricks onto a truck and the stench of the stinky tofu being cooked in a steaming wok on the street corner simply disappeared when I heard those words."

David had fought for a life and lost. It would not be the last time. He had so wanted to save the life of little Rose and he had failed. "People often ask me about the moment when International China Concern began. It was the very moment that I heard that Rose had died."

Rose came to represent every abandoned baby that languished in China's welfare centres. "These precious children were no longer nameless, faceless babies. To me, each one became as Rose had been: a sacred life to be fought for. God used the heart-breaking experience of meeting and losing Rose to ignite a mission and vision in me."

International China Concern (ICC) was the response to that little girl. "What happened to her should never have happened, and I knew that God was telling me that it shouldn't happen to anyone else. I still think back to her perfect nose and fingers.

Whenever I think about the circumstances, I can see her perfect little face so clearly."

What David had seen and experienced impacted him on the deepest level and inspired fundamental questions as everything he believed was challenged. He believed in a just and loving God – but where was the justice and love for the children in that place? He believed that children were meant to experience their first days being loved by their parents, not wasting away in orphanages hidden away from the world.

Rose was born fighting for life… and had lost. Who was there to protect her, and the countless other children like her? "I had seen children grabbing gnawed bones off the ground, desperate, and fighting for the chance to get a morsel of meat. I felt utter sadness." He had never expected that children should have to fight for life, protection and love, and he couldn't understand why there were so few people to help.

He lay on his bed and these questions cascaded through his mind. As he began to drift off to sleep, he couldn't get any closer to the answers. The only thing that seemed to break through was a clear sense of God speaking to him. In the chaos of his mind, he felt God saying, "David, you're here; what will you do?"

"What will I do? What can I do?" The question remained unanswered as he fell into a fitful sleep.

CHAPTER 2

The Early Journey

Though he did not know it, David's involvement in the social welfare system in China came at a turning point for China's orphanages. In the following years, the abandonment of healthy baby girls would begin to fall sharply. It reflected the advent of technology, allowing illegal sex-selective abortions. In some cases, the government began to approve the birth of a second child in circumstances where the first child was female. This would encourage parents to keep their girls.

However, there was no decline in the abandonment of disabled children to welfare centres. The pressure on the system grew more intense as it was overwhelmed with children with complex and costly disabilities. A solution was desperately needed in order to first reduce the mortality rate in China's orphanages, and then to provide those children with a higher quality of life.

The Communist system held a strong welfare ethic and provided for abandoned and disabled children but Chinese orphanages were in a terrible state because the country had experienced decades of war and centuries of strife. There were no training programs, no social welfare professionals, and no resources. Even the doctors, who were lauded during the Cultural Revolution for travelling barefoot (*chijiao yisheng* 赤脚医生), were in reality farmers with a basic paramedic training. In this environment, it was all that the staff in a welfare centre could do to take the children in and house them for a short time. If the basic care was not sufficient to sustain life, care for the living became almost impossible.

The journey begins

Ironically, it was his career in banking that led David Gotts to go to church. "I decided to leave school at sixteen after a neighbour suggested that I apply for a job as a junior banker with Barclays Bank, with the chance of moving up the ranks. The more I thought about it the more it seemed a much more attractive proposition than finishing school and moving on to university."

The bank put David through banking, finance, and accounts training. "I remember sitting in a finance class and chatting with two fellow trainees. As we chatted, it became evident that there was something else in their lives, and it meant more to them than career or success. They shared how they were Christians. They talked of their church and Jesus in a way that I had never encountered before. Then they invited me to visit their church in Congleton, some nine miles from my home in Macclesfield, England."

David's parents had taken him to Sunday school in the local Anglican church until he was a teenager. "I had yawned through all the stories and the droning liturgy until I had been confirmed into the Anglican church. That was what my parents asked – then I promptly left! It seemed to have so little relevance to my daily life." Nevertheless David, with characteristic enthusiasm, accepted their invitation to go the very next Sunday to a church a hundred people strong, previously called the Congleton New Life Christian Fellowship.

David was surprised by the warm welcome he received as a newcomer to the church. "The people were welcoming, entertaining, devoted, loving, and fun – all at the same time. There were people my age that saw their faith as not only relevant but central to their lives. I looked at the faces of those in church, and I knew that they had a faith that went far deeper than anything I had experienced. My curiosity was piqued."

David's father, Alan, took him to the youth group midweek and to Congleton on Sundays, acting as taxi driver to the too-young-to-drive teenager. "There was no sudden or immediate conversion but I felt that I was being invited to get to know God. It awoke a hunger in me to explore. The more I read of God's love, Jesus' coming to earth to die for our sins, His death and resurrection, the more I was challenged. He said He was the way, the truth and the life; and I wanted to find out if He was what He claimed to be."

People were very open to answering his questions. "Not only had they been warm and welcoming but they showed me genuine love and care. It didn't take long before I realized that their love was a reflection of an even greater love that God had for me."

About three months into attending New Life Christian Fellowship there was a meeting about a community event. Several churches were preparing to go out into the streets of the town to talk about Jesus. One evening, just before heading into town, while some were excited and eager, others were nervous. "As I examined myself, I realized that a change had happened. I no longer saw God as distant and irrelevant. Before I knew what I was saying, I declared, 'Why would I be nervous if I believe this so deeply? People need to know!'"

A friend from the group drove him home that night and she tentatively asked about his "confession of faith". David affirmed that he knew for certain that a deep change had taken place. He not only believed in God, but he now had a relationship with Jesus. Jesus was now the centre of his life and he would never be the same again.

"As I lay in bed that night, I was both excited and nervous. Excited because of the realization of what was taking place in my life. Nervous because I had a sense that this journey was going to lead me away from banking. I didn't know where it would take me, and I wasn't sure that I was happy about it. Yet I knew deep down that the realization of the centrality of God was just the beginning."

He wasn't the only one who sensed this change. Jean Mclellan, in her forties at the time, mentored David at the youth group, and this important relationship is still in place a quarter of a century later. Jean says, "Almost as soon as David became a Christian, he was interested in serving in mission overseas. I have a vivid memory of hearing a sermon one Sunday morning about Caleb and Joshua and how they were *wholeheartedly* committed to the Lord.[2] When the minister asked for people to come forward for the spirit of commitment of Caleb and Joshua to come into their lives, David rose. I knew then that he had received the spirit of Caleb."

David progressed in his banking career but his calling had come that day. New Life Christian Fellowship was an exciting place to grow as a new Christian. The leaders were encouraging and gave opportunities for the younger members of the church to get involved in leadership. The stories learned at Sunday school came together. "I was grateful for the dedicated people who had invested in me and I envisioned myself becoming a youth pastor. After all, I was young, so what else could I do?"

As the days passed by, David's thoughts of being a youth pastor were replaced by a strong sense that God was asking him to lift up his eyes and look beyond the borders of his own nation. David sensed that God might be calling him to serve overseas and the more he thought about it, the more deeply he felt that he was being called in this direction.

But how do you get to be involved with an overseas mission if you've never been involved with one? The vision of an organization called Youth With A Mission (YWAM) intrigued him. The founder, Loren Cunningham, while a young man himself, had been given a vision of waves breaking against the shores of the continents. As the waves broke, they became young people moving out to share God's love. This vision of young people captivated David.

YWAM had bases in different parts of the world but David had only heard of those in Hawaii and England. Hawaii sounded more like a beach holiday than a mission opportunity. He could find a spiritual need anywhere but he was looking particularly for a place with urgent, serious, and practical physical needs. His desire to share God's love was mixed with a passion to help the "whole person".

"As I look back on that time, I can see how God was leading me step by step. Lao Zi, or Confucius, said that 'the journey of a thousand miles begins with a single step'. I could feel that the early steps were small. Later steps would be large and I had to take a deep breath before taking them."

One day a friend made an offhand comment. "Why don't you go to Hong Kong? YWAM has a team there." That was Step One.

Another friend recommended a book called *Chasing the Dragon*. David bought the book and read it avidly. It told the remarkable story of a young woman, Jackie Pullinger, called by God to share His love with drug addicts, prostitutes, and the Triads (Chinese mafia) in Hong Kong's Walled City. It fired his interest. Step Two.

"One morning, I came down the stairs in my parents' house and saw an envelope containing a newsletter from YWAM. It focused on a newly established organization called Mother's Choice." This was a safe place in Hong Kong for pregnant, unmarried women where they could have their babies instead of being shamed at home or pushed to have an illegal abortion. Step Three.

Hong Kong was being laid on David's heart, for it had both spiritual and practical needs. Step Four would be in faith – to travel from his home and family to an unknown and mysterious place.

Still unsure, David and his friend Dave Clarkson, who also had an interest in serving overseas, decided to go away on a weekend retreat to think and pray about their next step. They reached Abersoch, a seaside town on the tip of North Wales, and chilled in a café. "I sat down with Dave and said I felt that if God was going to speak to me about going to Hong Kong, then He would do it before tomorrow lunch!"

The next morning they returned to the café for breakfast, and he was leafing through a newspaper until he reached the TV page. "Then all of a sudden, it was like time stopped." The schedule listed a Channel 4 documentary to be shown that very night – "The Law of Love: Jackie Pullinger outlines her method of working with drug addicts in Hong Kong". He closed the paper, turned to his friend and said, "I think that God has just told me to go to Hong Kong!"

That night they sat in front of the small TV at their hotel, waiting impatiently. But Jackie's program did not appear. They went through the channels and turned back to the newspaper to find that the schedule was for another programming region. The newspaper shouldn't have even been in Wales. They had just enough time to arrange for David's dad to record it on videotape.

"God had placed that particular newspaper in that particular shop for me to buy it. It was like He had taken out an advertisement to give me confirmation, and to enable me to trust in the huge step of leaving England. I never doubted God's call to go after that."

Soon after, David and Dave said goodbye to their families and boarded a flight to the mysterious Far East.

The Pearl of the Orient

Hong Kong in the early 1990s was a culture shock for the uninitiated. Life moved at ninety miles an hour and the people moved faster. The buildings were higher, the smell of money was stronger, and nowhere else could you cut the oppressive humidity with a knife in quite the same way.

Their landing at Kai Tak Airport (as it was then) was exciting enough, as jumbo jets banked away from the mountain at the last second, seemingly threading their way through Kowloon's buildings, decorated with aerials and washing lines, to line up with the runway. Hong Kong was a double dose of excitement mixed with anticipation: fascinating, overwhelming and alien. The heat and humidity and their incredulity masked the fact that it was David's first time away from home.

They were dragged jetlagged from the airport by friendly YWAM-ers, their hosts playing travel guide to the new tourists. It was hard to take in the thousands of Chinese signs precariously overhanging the bus in Nathan Road as it journeyed through the city. The Star Ferry that links the Island for a few cents was, and still is, the best way to see the stunning Hong Kong Island skyline for the first time. The tall, glistening buildings broke the backdrop of the green mountains behind and the sky was as blue as blue could be, broken only by brilliant puffy clouds.

Finally the kind hosts led their exhausted guests into a taxi that sped to the YWAM base halfway up the Peak. "*Nei ho ma. Bolodo, sap ho*" (the address at 10 Borrett Road) were David's first words of Cantonese, the dialect of Chinese spoken in Hong Kong.

David immediately liked YWAM. "The base was an amazing old colonial building that reminded me of England, which was comforting as everything else seemed so different." Their hosts led the jetlagged pair through the building, and then into a basement to a small room with bunk beds.

"As I stepped into the dark, dungeon-like room, the home-sickness kicked in. What had I done? Was I mad leaving my job, my family, my home, my country, to come here?" He collapsed onto his bed into a humid, sweaty, restless sleep. Over tfhe following days the homesickness deepened as he learned that

Dave would be moving to another YWAM location in a different part of the city. "I found myself wanting to go home!"

David had to dig deep and trust God rather than wanting to run. As yet they knew no one but they did have three phone numbers that had been given to them in the UK.

"One by one, I called the three numbers. With every call I felt a little better. These strangers, about whom I knew very little, were warm, welcoming, and each invited me to visit their church that Sunday. It turned out that all three of these different contacts from different people went to the same church!"

In Hong Kong's small and hugely expensive property market, schools and hotels host churches each Sunday. The "two Daves" (as they became known) turned up at Glenealy School, which hosted the Ambassador Fellowship. It was a small gathering and a significant contrast to David's home church. The people he met were an unusual combination of comfortable, sophisticated businessmen, civil servants, police or military staff, teachers, elderly missionaries, and their families. David's church in Congleton, a contemporary community church, was lively with contemporary Christian songs, not hymns. The Ambassador by contrast was quiet and more traditional.

"After the service, I concluded that this church absolutely wasn't for me. I determined to seek out Jackie Pullinger's church – which I knew to be more like my own. However, I felt God remind me how three completely different people had given me three contacts in Hong Kong who were all part of this church. As I went back every week, I was able to look beyond the form of worship to the hearts of the people that I was worshipping with. They were wonderfully hospitable… something that made a huge impact on a homesick nineteen-year-old deeply committed to living for God."

David still counts Ambassador International Church (as it is now called) as his "home church" in Hong Kong. Those different-from-him people became firm friends. That congregation was to provide some of the strongest and most loyal supporters of ICC and David personally.

On the Monday, the two Daves went their different ways; Clarkson to his School of Biblical Studies in a New Territories village; and Gotts retraced his steps across the harbour to Kowloon. David was about to start YWAM's Discipleship Training School (DTS). The first three months of this five-month course were held at the High Rock Christian Centre near Shatin, a new city in the New Territories of Hong Kong. The last two months were to be spent somewhere in Asia as field training.

David's train travelled over Boundary Street into the New Territories, through the tunnel under the famous Lion Rock Mountain, Shatin. From there the bus took him to High Rock. This was an imposing colonial brick-built building on the top of a commanding hill in the Shatin Valley. It had begun as a British police station in 1924 and has since seen service as a Japanese army command post, the Shatin Children's Home, and a school for the girls of wealthy families. YWAM had recently taken it over for discipleship training.

The comfort levels in the cells of the old police barracks had not improved in the intervening sixty-five years, as eight men lived in what had been turned into a basement dormitory. "It was still a step up from the dungeon I had been staying in immediately after my arrival! I introduced myself to some of the guys I was sharing with in the old police cell. We were all struggling with the accommodation but, as we got to know one another, a great camaraderie developed – and quickly it didn't seem so bad."

Not long after he arrived, he met a couple who worked with Mobile Mission Maintenance (MMM), an Australian charity that carried out construction projects for other charities. "Little did I know that getting to know them would give me one of the most important contacts to develop ICC. The time spent in classes was a learning feast!"

Each day would begin with worship and prayer followed by lectures. Teachers from around the world shared their experiences about working for disadvantaged communities in the field. Most were missionaries doing the kind of work to which David aspired. "We learned how to be people of faith, how to discern God's voice, and how to live with uncertainty, differences, danger, and disease in different countries and cultures."

The calling

David immediately connected with YWAM's values. "It was a profound and life-changing experience that still informs how I live my life today." He took to the training so well that YWAM approached him at the tender age of nineteen to lead one of the two-month outreach teams that were heading to Thailand. But a few weeks before he was due to set off, David realized he had to decline the invitation; he had heard the voice of God more clearly than ever before calling him to Mainland China. During a worship service he had heard an almost audible voice saying, "Pick up your pen and notebook and write down what I am going to tell you." Within seconds, he had scribbled down three things that God had put on his heart:

1. "I am calling you to go to China."

2. "I will use you to mobilize people to go to China."

3. "I will use you to train people to serve in China."

"So clearly did God speak to me that it gave me goose bumps, but as His words sank in, my first reaction was to see my own inadequacy. I was nineteen years old. I could certainly accept that God was calling me to China – but I couldn't possibly imagine how He could *use* me. It seemed impossible. But I knew *God* had spoken and so it wasn't about whether I thought I could do these things; it was about whether He felt He could do those things through me."

The worship continued around David as he accepted this calling to China. He would have to lay that call to mobilize and to train people before God in humility and prayer. If those things were meant to be, then He would bring them about.

It was as though David had found his compass heading. It was the certainty of this call that led him to turn down leading the outreach to Thailand. And it was this same certainty that filled him with excitement at the thought of two months in China. His commitment was to look and learn as much as he possibly could to equip himself for the challenges ahead.

Slow boat to China

The slow boat to China crept out of Hong Kong harbour on 3 December 1990 and steamed for three days along the coast toward Shanghai. With the romanticism of youth, David loved the idea of arriving into China in the same way as the missionaries of old. Flights into China were still largely for diplomats, businessmen, and rich, adventurous tourists.

This boat had one class – cattle class. The lower deck was a massive dormitory filled with bunks for 200 people. David would lay awake listening to snoring and spitting and getting first-hand experience of how the sheer number of people in China removes any real chance of privacy.

It also provided three days for David to reflect on his calling and his training. His certainty about China remained, but so did his concerns. "Is this the right place for me? Why not somewhere I know better? China is a Communist country; the police are powerful and scary and are said to throw followers of Jesus into jail. What if I go to China and don't like it?"

These questions swirled around in his mind but then he reasoned, "If I have been called to go to China, then I'll be OK. If God has asked me to do it, I have to lean on Him and trust my firm conviction. I just knew it was right." As he lay there a peace descended on him.

He stood at the rail of the ship, just as two years later he was to stand at the gate of the orphanage, with a sense of expectation. As they sailed down the Huangpu River, the air was still cold from the night sky but the Bund could be seen appearing through the mist.

The city was not as today with huge buildings left and right along the river. It was the Bund of the 1930s and the eastern side was paddy and swamp. But it looked beautiful. After so long in the planning and anticipation, at last this was David's first sight of Mainland China.

That first sight of China has affected many of its visitors. Some have hated it, some have loved it, some have taken it in their stride, but even the best prepared have not been able to anticipate what adventures it might bring. Like the challenges that faced Caleb and Joshua, China was daunting, huge, crowded, and seemed like a land full of giants.[3] But it also seemed like the Promised Land – though filled with tea and noodles rather than milk and honey.

David wanted to be realistic but was full of emotions: the absolute desire to be there, the sight of the Bund through the mist – it was like the cheesy missionary stories his friends joked about. But despite this, David's first thought as he sailed into Shanghai was, "This is my home."

David's time in China was everything he had hoped it would be. The team travelled through Shanghai, Nanjing, Guilin, and into the autonomous region of Guangxi to the Dragon's Backbone rice terraces of Longsheng. David even felt like Caleb. He couldn't help but feel that he was in his Promised Land.

They went out to meet people on trains, buses, and in parks. "I didn't speak a word of Chinese, but that didn't stop me from making friends. The warmth of the Chinese people and their hospitality drew me in – reinforcing my love for the culture." There were also a few precious moments where he was asked about Jesus. "The spiritual hunger was profound. People were caught in a spiritual vacuum and thirsty to hear about the love of God."

Leaving China at the end of the two months was hard, but just like Caleb, David knew he would return to this Promised Land. He must however learn Mandarin Chinese (*Putonghua*) and the best place for that was not Hong Kong, but Taiwan. So, in October 1990, the two Daves immersed themselves in a language programme in a provincial Taiwanese city, Taichung.

It was a tough two-year programme with several hours of classes per day, plus as many hours as it took to complete his homework. David took to the language like a duck to water, with the fearlessness of youth and a natural ability to learn.

"In the early days, I would walk around the neighbourhood greeting people with the few words that I knew. With each passing week, I would add more words to my vocabulary and gradually conversations began and friendships grew. It was a very happy time, without some of the heavy burdens which I would face in the future."

David also learned to trust God to provide. He had enough money for accommodation and trips to the open-air food stalls but each coming month he had to trust that God would provide the money for his language school fees.

"Finally I went to let the school principal know that I didn't have the money to pay for my classes. I was embarrassed but I wanted to be upfront. The principal of the language school, Esther Wong, simply handed me a receipt showing that my fees had all been paid in full!" Paid for, in fact, by the school principal herself.

This confirmed to him that he was in the right place, preparing himself for the work. "By providing for all I needed, God confirmed my path and taught me lessons about trust that would be invaluable for the future work of ICC." There would soon be a time when he had to trust God to provide sums of US$20,000 or more, and eventually for budgets of millions of US dollars.

Toward the end of his Chinese language studies, David began to think about the next step. They had gathered a group of local believers and missionaries together to pray for China but he didn't have a clear idea of where in China he would go and knew that working opportunities were limited. He could teach English, continue to study Mandarin, or get involved in supporting the work of the church – but this would largely be outside China. None of these resonated. His desire was not only to meet spiritual needs, but also physical ones. "All I could do was pray that God would open a door for me."

His literal call came by telephone in October 1992. His YWAM DTS workmate, Chan Kit Ying, had joined Mother's Choice and was looking to assist with the very first adoptions out of China. She had met Dawn Gage who had been working single-handedly on the ground in an orphanage in South China for two years.

"Dave, I've been invited to work with Dawn. I'm off in two weeks. I've decided that rather than stay in Hong Kong and focus on adoptions I'm going to move to China to help these desperate babies. Will you please pray for me?" Before answering he felt a nudge from the Holy Spirit. "There is an opportunity here. Don't miss it!" It was time to use some of his new skills.

"Of course I'll pray for you. In fact, I'm going to do more. I'd like to come and visit!"

CHAPTER 3

Walking in the Footsteps

D avid Gotts was not the first person God had led to bring His love to the great nation of China, and the fight for the abandoned and disabled in China did not start with him. He merely continued the journey of countless others attracted by China's size and culture, its inventions, trade and customs, and with a desire to help and support the Chinese people.

He had read the stories of those who had been Christian hands and feet before him, many of whom paid the ultimate price and left their mortal remains in the red soil of China. They knew the risks of violence and tropical diseases, bringing their belongings in the coffin in which they expected to be buried. At one time, 80 per cent died within two years.

Key missionaries to China

Alopen was the first recorded missionary to China, arriving in the Chinese capital Chang'an (Xi'an today) in 635. The tolerant Tang dynasty enabled Christianity to survive in China for 200 years before persecution almost drove it to extinction. Mariners and merchants began to come to China in the 1500s, many from Europe with a Roman Catholic background, followed by Jesuits, who brought Western culture, education, science, and technology to China. Trade in China continued to increase throughout the 1700s, and with it, Protestant missionaries.

Robert Morrison arrived in China in 1807 and became the first translator of the Bible into Chinese and author of a Chinese dictionary for English speakers. These tasks took him twenty-five years, during which time Chinese people were strictly forbidden to teach their language to a foreigner, on pain of execution.

In the poetic way that history repeats itself, he was born in Morpeth in northern England – where over 200 years later ICC's first administrative centre was established. At the time, missionaries to China were not expected to ever return home. They brought dedication, courage, proficiency, and expertise to the country, working hard to love the Chinese people against determined opposition.

James Hudson Taylor arrived in China in the mid-1800s. Hudson Taylor was one of the great pioneer missionaries and founded the highly successful China Inland Mission (CIM) in 1865 (today's Overseas Missionary Fellowship, OMF), which in the 1930s was recruiting over 1,000 missionaries a year. Much of the growth of the church in China stems from the legacy of Hudson Taylor and those who served with the CIM. Taylor was to die in Changsha – a city at the heart of the ICC story.

The life story of Hudson Taylor made a great impact on David and deeply influenced him. "Taylor completely integrated himself into the culture and language. I was moved by his love for and commitment to the people of China through his determination to bring the message of God's salvation. Hudson Taylor was my hero and I made his approach mine, as to how I would serve in China. I hoped to walk in his footsteps."

The first missionary woman to arrive in China was Mary Ann Aldersley in 1843. She was single and a teacher. Such women, following this legacy of absolute faith in their calling, still overwhelm the field of development in China today.

The bitter civil war between China's Communist Party led by Chairman Mao Zedong and the Nationalists led by Generalissimo

Chiang Kai-shek came to an end in 1949 with victory for the Communists. It became increasingly difficult for foreigners to remain in China, so many moved the short distance to the British Crown Colony of Hong Kong, where the laissez-faire policy of the colonial administration allowed everybody a generous freedom of action.

It was of course only intended to be for a short time until the foreigners were allowed back into China, so they busied themselves where they were. The mass of young, hungry, and ambitious refugees gave them plenty of social work to do. But Mao did not die until 1976 and his eventual successor Deng Xiaoping's "open door" policy was not instituted until 1978, so the legacy of these missionaries can still be seen in the schools, hospitals, old people's homes, and welfare centres all over Hong Kong.

Around the time David arrived in Hong Kong, many of the founders of these projects were in their late seventies or early eighties and were leaving for an uncertain retirement. Most had worked selflessly for half a century for the people of a foreign land even after the borders of China had closed to them. In their lives they had sacrificed possessions, careers of high potential, and precious hours with loved ones – often never to see them again. They had sold everything to fund themselves because of a burning desire to serve God in China.

Generations of ordinary people had been called to this magnificent, powerful, and yet awkward country – giving their whole lives on a calling from God. In their hearts burned a passion to see His people cared for around the world, no matter how small, sickly, and insignificant they may seem. It was time for a new generation to take over and look at China itself, but so far work had been mostly limited to the smuggling of Bibles (which was not actually illegal).

Dawn breaks the cycle

Two years before David arrived at that first Chinese welfare centre, Dawn Gage stumbled across it by accident.

In December 1990, she stood in front of her class of university students. Dawn hadn't intended to be a teacher. She had come to China a year previously to live with the Zhuang people, a large minority ethnic group in Southern China. Her task to teach the Bible to this group had been too big from the start as Dawn and her friends could speak little Chinese, and the only Bibles directed toward the Zhuang people were written in Russian. She had signed up with her mission group in the US to live in China for two years so, to make the best of it, she decided to teach English at a local university.

It was December and Dawn decided to teach the story of Christmas. It was the first time many of her class had heard of it.

"*Lao shi* ["Teacher"], what do you do at Christmas time?" one of her students asked.

"Well, we tend to stay at home and have some family time," she said slowly and carefully so that the words were understood. "We give each other presents and then walk down the street to see our neighbours. Oftentimes we would walk down the street to the old people's home and sing them Christmas carols, give them gifts, and spend time with one another."

"That's so much fun!" the class said. "Can we do that at Christmas?"

"Absolutely!" said Dawn. "If you can find a nursing home, we'll go and sing Christmas carols to them."

Her young students had no idea what a nursing home was, or even if they existed in China – despite the fact that they were young members of the Communist Party – but they went out to look for one. It was deep into January 1991 when they came back victoriously to Dawn to tell her that they had managed to find one.

"Well, it's a little too late to sing Christmas carols," explained Dawn, "but it will be a good trip for the class, so let's go anyway."

They snaked through town on their bikes and ended up outside the Nanning Welfare Centre looking for some elderly people. They were met at the open gate by the staff who asked, "Have you come to see the children?"

Teacher and students were all surprised but in China a state welfare centre would look after both children and the elderly at the same site. Dawn's students had no idea such a place existed in their own city, but they were interested in going inside, and so they stepped through the circle-shaped gate – just a group of university students and their foreign teacher.

Dawn was shocked. What they encountered that day was horrific. As she walked through the rooms of the welfare centre, she encountered a hundred children aged from babies to teenagers.

Around sixty of the children were older than three; many were visibly disabled, sitting on the concrete floor, naked from the waist down. She saw children who were malnourished, neglected, and tied to potty chairs – ribs showing – as other children ran around them, undisciplined and uncontrolled.

Dawn walked into another room and discovered forty babies lying in cots. The majority were baby girls. The sight and smell had a penetrating impact on her, as it did on David when he came to visit.

Dawn noticed a smell that lingered over the whole building. She didn't understand what it was until her mother, a nurse, came to visit her a few years later. Carol recognized the smell of death from her experience of working with terminal patients in hospitals in America.

Dawn began to visit the orphanage regularly. She didn't know what she could do, but she knew she had to come up with something. She quickly realized that although there were always forty to forty-five babies in the baby room, each time she visited many would have been replaced. She realized that as babies died of illness or malnourishment, abandoned newborn babies would quickly take their place.

The neglect of children in the welfare centre was born out of a lack of understanding – of care, of knowledge, of the conditions up the chain of command, of budgets, and of the desperation of staff with no training in how to handle the circumstances. The staff were not cruel or malevolent, but they were hardened against the conditions that placed little value on yet another human life. Unlike David and Dawn, they were not motivated by a conviction that each life, each baby, each disabled child, each soul, was valuable.

Although Dawn's involvement in orphanage life came about by accident, she somehow felt at home in that place. Her father was a military pilot and had died when she was a young child. One of her early memories had been thinking that if anything happened to her mother she would be an orphan, so she declared to her mother that she wanted to be an "orphanist" – to look after orphans. It didn't surprise her that she ended up where she did.

Dawn had six months left of her two-year term in China, and she began to visit the welfare centre, becoming a huge hit with the kids. They came to love and cherish her weekly visits.

Each week Dawn would follow the same routine. On her arrival she would be met at the gate by a young boy whom she called "the doctor". He was deaf, but he had a special visual gift for noticing the sick children at the welfare centre. The young doctor would take her by the hand and lead her around the welfare centre to each child who was sick, or had a cut or a bruise.

She had no medical background, but Dawn would pay each child some special attention. She and the doctor would clean their wounds with an antiseptic wipe and cover them with a Band-Aid.

After her rounds, they would sing songs, or do a simple craft project. Dawn's students often came with her, and they would give out bananas and hard-boiled eggs to get some more nourishment into the children.

For Dawn, the most important aspect to her visits was that she was regularly present. She focused on building relationships with the children by spending time with them and she found that she was best suited to the older ones – those who were aged six to twelve – with whom she could chat easily.

At that time, she was able to freely walk in and out of the welfare centre. Security was minimal and after building trust with the caregivers, Dawn began to take a few children home at the weekends. They would walk to her house with three kids on her one bicycle. They loved to play in Dawn's bath, help to cook food and eat in a small group around a table, and take naps in a warm, comfortable bed. Their lives were ones of neglect, and with death all around them their one concern was survival. Where children should be able to take for granted a bath, a meal, a bed, and a family, to these children these things were luxuries that they couldn't have imagined.

Those precious times of pouring love into the children had a significant impact on Dawn. After six months, she knew she couldn't leave the kids and return home to America. She felt she couldn't say "I love you" to the children and then leave them. They deserved more than her words; they needed her to be present. Dawn felt they needed someone in their lives who would be there for them. As she continued to live in Nanning, and fell more in love with these children, she began to have a mother's heart, a fighter's heart.

Dawn often played with one particular tiny girl at the welfare centre; she was cute but had a big stomach distended by an infestation of worms. One week Dawn couldn't find her and after a desperate search she found her hiding under a bed, weak and in a helpless condition. Upset, concerned, and full of love for this child, she asked a local doctor if she could take the little girl to the hospital. "What would you want to do that for?" the doctor demanded. "If you take her there, you spend money, and when you bring her back she will only be in the same situation."

Dawn looked at the doctor and said: "I know. Why don't you just throw all the babies into the river, then they don't have to lie there and suffer?" The doctor was stunned. She didn't know whether to laugh, or feel embarrassed or humiliated. The scale of these issues in a country that had not long come out of decades of war was too big for ordinary people, even doctors, to fathom.

Dawn's outburst exemplified the stress, loneliness, and anger she was feeling. After her first eighteen months, she estimated that she saw 700 babies die at this one welfare centre.

She was trying hard to help them, and each week when she visited she would try to give attention to as many babies as she could. As she held each one and gave them a bath, she knew that for many of these precious children this would be the last time they were held before they died. Each week Dawn would come home from the welfare centre and stare at the wall for hours. She herself was becoming numb; she was feeling dead inside from the effort of processing what she was witnessing.

One day, when she was in the baby room holding a baby who she knew wouldn't live until her next visit, she looked out of the window into the courtyard and saw some of the older children playing. She realized that the next time she came to the orphanage, those children she watched playing would still be there. Dawn speculated that these children had been abandoned after a few years of living with their families. They were more able to survive the harsh life in the welfare centre than newborn babies were.

After months of trying to help the babies Dawn admitted that she couldn't do anything. She never thought of just taking one or two babies home to give them a chance of a life and a future; she was trying to think of a bigger solution.

With a baby in her arms and her eyes on the older children in the courtyard, Dawn dedicated the babies to the Lord, and with them her role in their lives. She asked the Lord to send someone else in to help the babies, and she decided she would begin to focus all of her time and energy on helping the older children – an investment which would lead her to found a school and to support an orphanage for older kids, Living Stones Village, a few years later.

Kit Ying establishes a work

Dawn's prayers were answered in the summer of 1992 when she met Chan Kit Ying in Hong Kong. Kit Ying shared her vision to set up foster care and adoption projects. Dawn had a perfect site at the Nanning Welfare Centre.

Kit Ying had recently returned with a degree in social work after studying in Canada and had been working with pregnant teenage girls and their babies in Hong Kong with Mother's Choice. She was deeply drawn to China and, having recently completed the same YWAM DTS and been in the same China field trip group as David Gotts, was looking for ways to work in the country.

Shortly after meeting Dawn, Kit Ying took her first trip into China on her own. Aware of the situation at the orphanage, she prepared herself for what she would see. She intentionally went in as a calm observer, despite the horrors she encountered. She remembers being focused on the needs and was ready to move forward to do what was needed. She had a deliberate desire to get things done, and after a few observational visits, she was drawn to a small baby who needed some extra attention.

Kit Ying spoke good Mandarin and went to the welfare centre director to ask if she could take the baby to hospital. The director said that she could, but also said, "Why not take an older one? After all, babies are such *ma fan* [trouble] to look after." Kit Ying allowed herself a lie: "Don't worry, I know all about how to look after babies." She walked out of the orphanage with a baby in her arms and hailed a *san lun che*.

She asked the driver to take her to a supermarket, where she found some baby formula and returned to her hotel room. She changed and bathed the baby and put her down to sleep. While the baby slept, Kit Ying looked down at her and for the first time that day she began to panic: "What on earth have I done? I have a baby right here and I have no idea what to do with her! What if she dies? There is no way I can look after this baby!"

Still, she continued to focus on the task in hand. Instead of returning to Hong Kong after those three days, Kit Ying stayed in Nanning. She learned to change nappies and took some more babies from the orphanage back to her hotel. Soon, her hotel room had become a baby room. She made friends with all of her neighbours and asked each family if they would be able to take care of a baby. Soon babies who would otherwise have died in the orphanage were instead living with sweet and loving families in the local community.

From the first time she walked out of the orphanage with a baby Kit Ying was acutely aware of the lack of policy to protect the little ones. As a qualified social worker, she couldn't believe she had been allowed to take even one child directly from the orphanage, with no paperwork, training, or background checks. She wanted to set an example of appropriate foster care and adoption to the Chinese welfare system so she arranged a meeting with the civil affairs bureau in Nanning to present a proposal for establishing international adoption procedures.

Although she had experienced working with the adoption process in Hong Kong and had helped to arrange seven adoptions in another province in China, she still felt like a young, inexperienced foreign woman in a different country. She didn't know how to behave in China, she wasn't aware of many laws and policies, but she was so focused on providing some kind of solution to such a need that she pushed through her concerns. To her amazement, the government official she met at the civil affairs bureau turned out to be a key official with the authority to approve adoptions.

With her first baby living in her hotel room, she phoned a friend from an adoption agency in Hong Kong to tell them about the infant. Within days, the little girl was matched with an American family who were already in the process of adopting a child from China. In September 1992, just one month after she arrived at the orphanage, the first two babies had been adopted. In her first three months, she had pushed the number up to fourteen.

All of the babies Kit Ying encountered at the beginning were healthy baby girls who died unnecessarily. At the time, there was a 100 per cent mortality rate for new babies who arrived at the orphanage. Thirty to forty babies were brought in each month, and none were able to survive in those conditions. Healthy babies died from dehydration, from not learning how to suck, from exposure, or from choking on their milk when prop-fed from a bottle that could roll away, leaving the baby unfed. From a future of certain death at the orphanage, these babies were surviving simply because they had access to basic care and love. Now, with the model of the babies in her hotel room and those in foster families who were surviving and being adopted, the welfare centre began to take notice.

One day the director showed her to an empty apartment inside the orphanage compound and said: "This room is for you." Kit Ying remembers being shocked. What had begun as a short visit to an orphanage now looked as if it was expanding into something more permanent. She was a single girl working alone, without an organization or a team. No one was forcing her to be there; she remembers the decision was between her and God. She lived one day at a time, and each day she chose to stay and serve the babies.

After a few months in Nanning, she returned to Canada to see her family. She had to make a decision about whether to officially immigrate to Canada as her parents and siblings had done. She had grown up in a loving family, in a comfortable home, but she couldn't forget what she had seen. She knew this meant her life would be different from the lives of her peers in their twenties, but she couldn't pretend that she didn't know what was happening to these babies. She returned to China because she knew that these babies needed her; she had to keep moving forward, pushing through. There was no turning back.

Now that she was living in the orphanage, the situation was much more intense. She felt that she was in an emergency room. Each day she would go to the orphanage baby room and look at the babies. If she thought a baby could survive a few more days, she left them. If a baby looked as if they wouldn't survive the night, she took them.

The work didn't get easier, but Kit Ying persisted, feeling that she was given supernatural strength – and health – to continue. When other foreign volunteers came to the orphanage to visit, they would inevitably return home with lice or scabies, but Kit Ying never got sick.

Her friend, mentor, and key supporter, Helen Stephens, the managing director of Mother's Choice in Hong Kong, would visit her and bring Kit Ying back to Hong Kong at regular intervals for a break. Helen allowed Kit Ying to sit for hours without talking, dealing with experiences so extreme that it took time to process.

Kit Ying thought long and hard about how she was going to survive in the midst of such suffering. She needed the prayers of those who knew and loved China and would stand with her in her work and she remembered her friend, David Gotts. He had shared his love for China on their YWAM programme. He was studying Chinese in Taiwan and might be able to help.

So Kit Ying gave him a call…

CHAPTER 4

Making a Commitment

C hina was unique and David could only follow his nose. You can have no plan in mind when there is no blueprint to follow. He was in uncharted territory. It was overwhelming. There was so much to think about for a twenty-one-year-old about to embark on a path that had not yet been formed.

Straight after his orphanage visit, David flew to Hong Kong. Rose's face was imprinted on his heart. He would have liked to forget what he had seen but not that little girl whose life he had tried to save. "Faces would look shocked as I related the experience. Eyes would fill with tears as I talked about the babies and children. People would say, 'I just didn't know.' It was as if their eyes had been opened and with that came a strong urge to help."

One conversation in particular opened up a range of possibilities. By 1993, Richard Hubbard had already been into China several times with a group called Chinese Church Support Ministries (CCSM), and with its founder, Ross Paterson. Richard and David sat down in the coffee shop at the Kowloon YMCA. The café was busy and noisy, but could have been as quiet as a library as David began to ask questions.

What could they do that was useful? What were the obstacles? How would the Chinese government react to an offer of help? Could David use the resources and experience of CCSM while developing his own?

They threw around ideas of how to start a project – the kind of conversation familiar to all entrepreneurs embarking on a new venture.

David quickly brought up the idea of sending teams into China to work in the welfare centre, which was the YWAM tradition. Richard agreed that he could help David organize their trip to China under CCSM's name. He already knew how to organize the permissions and make the general arrangements needed; a vital but complicated step, especially when international phone calls and the postal system were patchy and unreliable.

David talked to friends and mentors about mobilizing people with a heart to serve the abandoned children of China but it needed more than just a few like-minded individuals. Regular big teams, including healthcare experts, would have more pairs of hands to hold more babies, and more pairs of feet to do something useful within the Chinese system.

"I already knew that my initial vision to help these children went further than just helping the babies at the orphanage for a few weeks every few months. I could see that the team approach might be a means of building relationships, credibility, and trust with the welfare centres – and with the government."

Most transactions in China are built upon relationships and David felt strongly from the start that this work must be in partnership with the government and that they must be completely open in order to build that trust.

Their approach was to come in the spirit of servanthood, to do what was needed, without criticism of the system or of any of the staff or officials. Despite the terrible conditions they saw within the orphanages, they knew that if they spoke out in the wrong manner, it would damage their relationship with the government.

"I believed that lasting change could only come through influencing by example, by showing the transformation that can take place in an abandoned and disabled child's life when they are loved, nurtured, given opportunities to learn and to reach their full potential."[4]

It was decided that the first team would go into China in July 1993. That sounded easy but it took a long six months to plan the strategy. The time merely intensified David's mental struggle with the immensity of the challenge ahead, as he wrestled with questions: "Can I make a difference in this situation? Is it possible for me to bring change? Do I want to work amidst death and suffering? Who would? Do I want to dedicate my life to something so hidden away? Is it worth making a difference to just one or two children? Will anyone respond or even care?" David's long months of wrestling with God about giving himself to this work continued as he prepared to lead the first team into Guangxi Province.

The first team

That first team consisted of thirteen people who went to the orphanage for twelve days. They gathered team members by calling on their friends in Taiwan and Hong Kong, many of whom agreed to come upon asking. The party was rounded out by a group of students from northern England's Durham University Christian Union.

It took a while, as always, for flights, buses, hotels, passports, visas, and local permissions to be finalized but finally this disparate group of twenty to twenty-two-year-olds met on a typical steamy-summer July night in Hong Kong with the temperature well into the thirties and the humidity touching 100 per cent. Everyone was shower-wet by the time they had walked from their hotel to the restaurant. It was a relief to dry off in the air conditioning as they introduced themselves at what was to become a traditional first night team dinner.

The trip was life-changing for these young adults away from home in a strange land. Travelling in China itself was an adventure and, once they arrived and began work in the welfare centre, they had no rest for two weeks, even back at their noisy and uncomfortable hostel. Being the middle of summer, everyone was hot and sweaty; the children in the orphanage had heat rashes and nappy rashes that left deep weals on their skin. Every room was overpowered by the smell of milk, cooking, coal smoke, and urine. "I looked on as babies died in the arms of university students from comfortable middle-class England."

They did not have the age or experience to make any of the key decisions that they had to make. They simply did their best, used common sense, and followed their instincts, but were utterly overwhelmed.

Despite the horrors around them, this first team returned to the orphanage every day without criticizing the system, arguing with the directors, or telling caregivers what to do. They did not have the outlet of someone to blame and so they put everything they had into caring for the children, believing their example would slowly make an impact on the staff and directors of the orphanage. As they served, they did not speak out unless their opinion was invited. Where they had an opportunity, they would use it as a way to gently train the caregivers to use appropriate methods of care.

Where they saw abuse and neglect, they brought love and care rather than accusation – though the latter option was tempting, particularly to those who had a strong sense of justice. They knew that the focus of this initial time was not to bring lasting change; it was to invest, give, and build a foundation of trust. They recognized that until they had set an example of continued, loyal commitment to the children, they did not have a right to speak out.

What did come easily was to love the children. Divided into twos and threes, each small group would take a section of the orphanage: the babies, the toddlers, the pre-teens, or the teens. They would hold the children, hug and play with them, make faces, sing and pray, bathe, clean, and change nappies. They would hold their faces or stroke their hands to stimulate circulation.

They untied children from potty chairs and gently carried them outside to sit in the sun to see the sky. They mixed milk formula, wiped noses, and got covered in sweat as well as all kinds of body fluids. The team did anything they could think of to stimulate the children physically or mentally so that their eyes would begin to flicker with recognition. They gave everything they had. No one sat on the sidelines. They stuck together, supported one another, rallied round each other as each team member inevitably had a low point. They prayed together, they encouraged one another; the power of the team was ever present.

With a focus on serving and without the scope to criticize, the team began to empathize with the caregivers and orphanage workers. At first it was easy to see them as uncaring and heartless as they watched babies die daily, but they began to see the other point of view. The orphanage was understaffed, and they did not have time to give each child the care and attention they needed. With just one or two staff members per room, they only had the time and energy to prop a bottle near a child's mouth and change their nappies routinely – or in most cases the newspaper substitute.

They couldn't revolve their work around the needs of the children, considering when each child was hungry, or when each one needed to be changed. The team began to see why the caregivers left the children to cry on their own. If they picked up crying babies, they would learn that their cries would be heard, and they would continue to cry. It was easier to let the babies realize for themselves that their cries would not be answered, and the team understood why the orphanage was so silent, void of the usual noises babies and children make.

Struggles of the heart

That first trip was a mind-blowing experience for all concerned, but coming down from the mountaintop was not going to be easy. David had learned so much during these two weeks, and some of his questions had been answered, but in other areas, the experience had led to more confusion. David continued to struggle with his future.

"Am I up to it? Do I want to do it? Would I make a difference? How costly would it be if I were to devote my young life to this? Can we resolve any more of the uncertainties?"

Still struggling several months later, David decided to have a weekend away and spent an October Friday afternoon crossing the rugged and beautiful Taiwanese mountains to Hualian on the east coast. The next morning he was by himself in the hotel lobby when he felt the full burden of his struggle. He sank into a chair and prayed, "I can't do it; it's too much to ask."

It was then that he felt God saying to him, "You can't. You are not enough… but I can. You give yourself to it and I'll bless it. But if you decide to do something else, I'll bless that too."

David had come to the point where the decision was not dependent on the questions he had been asking. He knew that if he was willing to give himself up to the unknowns of the future, then God would be in the midst of it. He was already willing to serve in whatever role God had in store for him. It was the commitment itself that he had struggled with. And here was God telling him that it was his decision and whatever path he decided to take, God would bless that way.

He felt freedom in this clear message. He knew that this was now his choice, and he could go in any direction. He sensed that God was inviting him to be a part of this work, not demanding it of him. David said, "I choose to do this," and the burden was lifted from his shoulders. This was what he was going to do.

"This was a very important understanding of what God was asking of me," David said later. "We are now into the third decade of ICC and we've faced some very difficult times. If I had felt that God had forced me down that road, I would not have been able to persist. It was not the case that God forced me into a hard situation. God gave me the freedom to choose my path. Eventually, I chose freely to commit myself to China because of my love for Him. After that there was never a time when I resented what He had called me to do, because it was I who had chosen it."

That moment in October 1993 was catalytic for David. From then on, he knew what he was going to do – but making the decision didn't automatically make everything easier.

CHAPTER 5

Where is Changsha?

Now that David had made the decision to move forward, he began to think about his approach and strategy for longer-term work in Chinese orphanages. "I wanted to share God's love, particularly with those children who had been pained by abandonment just because they were disabled." However, he knew that this could only be done through meeting their tangible needs.

They only had one approach: David – and whoever would join him – would seek to love and care for the children by working with servant hearts. They could inspire change by sharing their Christian values in their work. Evangelizing could not be the focus, for that was something that the Chinese government would struggle to accept. David remembered the words of St Francis of Assisi: "Preach the gospel at all times. And when necessary, use words."

The first team had learned that individuals in China were viewed with little value. Government partnerships were formed between institutions. David felt that they must form an organization to present themselves, like a formal company with a solid identity, a brand, an official address, a board of directors, and business cards. "If the vision that I carried could be expressed under the umbrella of an organization that brought together ideas, resources, and people... well, that might enable us to get a hearing."

One evening, David and his American friends Tim and Carmen Tyler bounced names for the company off each other. "The word 'concern' stood out – because that's why we were there. We felt that we were being called to serve China's children. 'International' sounded impressive – and something the government would respect!" By the end of dinner, International China Concern (ICC) was officially born.

Even the Chinese name, a mouthful at *Guoji Guanxiao Zhongguo Cishan Xiehui* (国际關小中国慈善协会) appeared that evening. ICC was later shortened to a more captivating *Ai Xi Hui* (爱希会), the short form of "love, hope, and opportunity", and this became the tagline of the future ICC.

The next team was scheduled to arrive in January 1994, and David began to work hard to organize it. But in the months leading up to it, China's acceptance of foreigners had darkened dramatically, jeopardizing their future team's work. In late 1993, an article appeared in Hong Kong's *South China Morning Post*, highlighting the plight of orphans and disabled children in China, and focusing on the "Dying Rooms".

The article prompted a wave of international criticism of China's orphanages. It particularly highlighted the very orphanage where they had been working – and where they were planning to send another team in less than a month. Accusations between foreign workers arose. Dawn Gage found herself being accused of leaking information to reporters – even before she had read the article for herself. The Nanning orphanage, which had always been open and welcoming to outsiders, now shut its doors firmly, refusing to let anyone inside.

David felt relieved that the opportunity to return to the orphanage had closed. He still had a gnawing doubt about his ability to lead the trip. He struggled with the lack of control he felt going into a country where anything could change at the last minute. That initial step of faith in Hualian did not turn him into a spiritual giant overnight. It was a small step on a long journey that continues today. He was still nervous about the path ahead. Despite having committed to doing this work, it seemed too hard, too much, too difficult, too big. If he was that relieved not to go back to China's welfare centres, then maybe he couldn't do it after all.

The closed doors of the orphanage seemed to be a way out. He emailed CCSM's founder and director, Ross Paterson, telling him of the closed doors and his intention to cancel the team. Unexpectedly, Ross challenged David, "Why not go anyway, and see what God does?" The tickets were booked, and the team was still coming from as far apart as Australia and Taiwan. Somewhat reluctantly, David agreed that the trip would continue.

Looking back on it, he remembers it as a time of learning. "In our humanity, we feel inadequate and lacking in strength. But if by faith we are willing to venture into the unknown, we must trust that God is in the midst of it."

The map

A few weeks later, the second team led by the two Daves officially became the first ICC short-term team, although CCSM had given them their support. The global press stories and the lockdown on orphanages across China meant that the trip began with a sense of the unknown. The "Team to Nowhere" all met up in the city of Guangzhou. "We sat in the hotel room without contacts, leads, or plan. All we could do was pray and ask God to lead us wherever He chose."

Before they prayed, a team member placed a map of China on the floor and the whole team sat and knelt around it. They asked God where He would have them go. As they knelt down for a closer look, the whole of China lay before them. The options were enormous, from Tibet and Xinjiang in the west, to Dalian next to

North Korea in the northeast, to Yunnan, which is closer to India than Beijing.

"My heart quickened as I looked around at the faces of those around me and I asked whether anyone had sensed God's leading. I had a name that had dropped into my mind previously – but it was a place that I knew nothing about. At first, I didn't want to say anything – it might be a risk that could lead us nowhere." All the same, David moved his finger across the map and tapped over a city in the middle of China. "This was the name that had dropped into my mind – it was the city of Changsha."

But where was Changsha? It turned out that it was not too far away, about 700 kilometres (430 miles) to the north, the provincial capital of Hunan Province. It is famous for hot food, thick succulent pork dishes, and for being the birthplace of Chairman Mao Zedong, the first Communist leader of China – so they couldn't be sure of a liberal welcome at the station. However, the team were now certain that they were no longer the team to nowhere.

The next morning they met up at Guangzhou railway station, fought their way through the shouting, jostling, impatient, bag-laden crowds to the ticket counter and booked twelve hard sleeper tickets to Changsha.

The train journey crept at a snail's pace overnight: a fifteen-hour trip that would take two and a half hours by bullet train today. They arrived in the early morning on a typical Changsha day. It was cold, wet, noisy, smoky and unwelcoming, and they had nowhere to stay. They had no contacts in the city, so the team split up. Half of them went to find a hotel, while the other half began to look for a welfare centre.

Introduction to Changsha

The hotel group found that nearly all the accommodation was not licensed to take foreigners. Eventually they found somewhere, booked in, and settled in their rooms. They had only been there half an hour when they were asked to pack up and leave. Foreigners were so rare in Changsha that even the front desk didn't know the rules. It was only when their passport details had reached the Public Security Bureau that the hotel itself found that foreigners were unable to stay. Welcome to China!

The receptionist handed back the passports and pointed them in the direction of another hotel down the road. They wandered northward up the traffic-laden street and found the Liu Fang Hotel. The cost of the room was way over budget, the price being inflated because they were foreigners. The team was getting tired and their patience was running out. When the usual negotiation failed to win a lower price, the team sat down and refused to leave until they had a better offer.

The hotel realized it had a group of stubborn foreigners on its hands and eventually agreed a satisfactory price with, as is normal in China, both sides feeling they had got the best end of the bargain. The hotel was a shabby two star establishment where everything smelt of cigarette smoke and the carpets were sticky and clicked when stepped upon. Complex organisms lived under the bed.

The water leaked from the pipes in the bathroom and strayed onto the bedroom carpet, giving the air a rotten damp smell, which combined unpleasantly with the previous guest's cigarette smoke. The beds were hard and felt none too clean. Yet the Liu Fang was to become the go-to place for ICC teams and staff in Changsha for many years afterwards.

Each night the hotel's bellboy would thoughtfully slip the business cards of scantily clad ladies-of-the-night under the door. The telephone would often suddenly ring in the middle of the night. The first time this happened one of the Australian visitors picked up and heard, in broken English, "Messagee, messagee!"

Struggling to understand, but wondering and concerned about the message and who it was from, all he could say was,

"Yes." Ten minutes later, a pretty young woman knocked on the door to offer him massage services. David quickly called down to the reception and made sure that there would be no more calls offering "messagees".

The other half of the team had been searching all day for an orphanage without success. Welfare centres were often built on the outskirts of cities, hidden away from public view, so that parents considering abandoning a child would not know where to go. Of course, children were then left at railway and bus stations.

Just as they were on the verge of giving up for the day, a very experienced Chinese-speaking Taiwan-based American team member had the bright idea to just go to the Civil Affairs Bureau and ask whether the "International China Concern" team could work in the city's welfare centre for the next ten days.

David was horrified. "My first reaction to this crazy idea was to say no. Foreigners were obviously not welcome at welfare centres at this time of lockdown. It seemed that going straight to the government was a short cut to spending time in a Changsha police station before being deported to Hong Kong. On the other hand, we had little choice… We had to trust that if God had led us to this city, it was hopefully for more than just the Liu Fang Hotel."

Against all odds, and to the surprise of everyone involved, the plan worked perfectly. They were promised an introduction to the director of the No. 1 Welfare Centre of Changsha the next morning. Perhaps it was just to see the few foreigners who came to the city, or perhaps because it was even more astounding to have a group of foreigners in the interior of China looking for orphans – but the director actually came to see for himself.

There was a hush as Director Zhou appeared at the door, a big man, imposing in his heavy Chinese army green padded greatcoat. "He was intimidating. Ex-military and in his forties he had been sent to become head of the children's and elderly social welfare centre in Changsha. I was only twenty-two and relieved that I had two experienced team members from Taiwan with good Mandarin to do the talking."

The director sat in the only chair of the hotel room while the ICC team perched on the bed. He listened silently while they explained that they were from an international NGO and were looking to partner to help disabled children in China's welfare centres. They were careful to emphasize that the team only wished to improve the lives of the children and to support the welfare centre in their work.

David shared that they were looking to return several times a year with teams. The room fell silent as David's pitch concluded and they braced themselves for a rejection. The recent bad publicity about orphanages must have reached Changsha.

Director Zhou broke the silence. "Welcome to Changsha. We would like you to come to care for the children and we are happy to let you work at our welfare centre. I will send you a bus to your hotel at eight o'clock tomorrow. Goodbye." He then got up, nodded, and walked out.

Changsha Welfare Centre

This initial meeting was the beginning of an excellent eight-year relationship with Director Zhou until his retirement. God had not only led ICC to Changsha but had opened a door. The team members were elated; just a day earlier they had been staring at a map of China not knowing where to go – and tomorrow morning they would be meeting the children they couldn't wait to serve. More importantly, it was the beginning of a strong relationship between ICC and the government of China.

The first day at the welfare centre was a shock to many. Most of the team members had never experienced life in a Chinese orphanage and gasps could be heard as they walked around from room to room. They could not comprehend the dirty rooms of chronically ill and neglected children.

Team members held dying babies as they breathed their last breath. Those with disabilities were carefully fed. The emotionally disconnected were loved until their dead eyes flickered with the will to live. To love meant opening one's heart, often to have it broken. For many of the children, death would not wait for long.

Late-night tears flowed and some found it hard to contain their anger. It laid a burden on their hearts and they just prayed that they could make some kind of difference – no matter how small. But for now, they had to put their personal feelings behind them and concentrate on spending time with babies, toddlers, and older children.

They recognized that it took a significant amount of trust for the director to welcome them, so David and the team concentrated on coming into the orphanage with uncritical, servant hearts. Every word and deed had to lead toward building a solid relationship, for only this would convince the director and his superiors that ICC could help to transform the children's lives and the institutional system in which they lived. Their actions had to speak louder than their words.

It was during this trip that David realized that God had given him a heart to love and serve babies and children. He remembered how much he had loved kids when he was younger, and even changing nappies, making up milk formula, feeding babies, and playing for hours with the children brought him real joy. Young as he was, David was already seen as the team leader, but he really wanted to be simply another pair of hands trying to make a difference.

Some of those children that ICC connected with on that first trip to Changsha would feature throughout ICC's early history, working their way into the hearts of the team members. Chen Shi, Li Shi, Sun Wu, Tang Xiao Kun, Wang Gui, Wang Hua, Wang Wu,

Yang Lan, and Zhou Li, as well as many others, quickly became part of the ICC family.

The ICC team workers became parental role models to those children, many of whom have gone on to pursue careers as effective members of the community, despite their disabilities. The experience also opened Director Zhou's heart and after his eventual retirement he continued to work with disabled children, even attending ICC's twentieth anniversary celebrations in May 2013. ICC's relationship with the Changsha No. 1 Welfare Centre continues to this day.

The thought of leaving the children at the end of the trip was hard and the team members worried about their survival after they had gone. So ICC began to bring in teams every three months as people responded to David's talks on the challenges of the Chinese welfare system at churches around the world.

David found that the logistics and management of the trips demanded more of his attention. Rather than feed and play with the children, his days at the welfare centre were spent walking from room to room, checking on groups, answering questions, solving problems, helping with translation, and sorting out travel and accommodation. He was beginning to be faced with a choice: to be a pair of hands holding babies, or to be a pair of hands that would facilitate twenty team members holding babies. "It was a painful realization. I loved spending time with the children and knew that I would miss that. However, the vision that the lives of more children could be transformed was too strong. And I felt that God was asking me to organize the trips."

ICC's every growth spurt would now push David further away from the children and more into organizational and business management. It was a natural progression. He recalled the second and third part of his mission calling: that he would be used to mobilize people to go to China, and that he would train people to work there independently.

International China Concern was not about him but about the formation of an organization of which he was only a tiny part – but whose future he could influence.

CHAPTER 6

A Pine in the Wasteland

David organized two-week teams that went into the Changsha No. 1 Welfare Centre every three months of 1994. Each team encountered the same overwhelming circumstances of high mortality rates, but they persevered, continuing to love the children and their caregivers.

They gradually noticed small improvements but, as with orphanages across the nation, the Changsha Welfare Centre was underfunded and understaffed, and systemic problems remained. It seemed there was a bottomless pit of need.

"We began to realize that even with frequent trips to the welfare centre we could only scratch the surface... but at least they were a means of gaining their trust. What we needed was a permanent presence to make a real impact; a long-term partnership that would enable us to stem the rates of mortality and present our values."

After several team visits David and some Taiwan-based friends raised with Director Zhou the subject of making their visits more permanent. He was open to the idea, although a foreign presence in his welfare centre made him nervous. "Then in January 1995, Director Zhou asked me whether we had ever considered doing long-term projects in Changsha. Not wanting to seem too eager, I carefully said that ICC would like to and asked if we could continue the discussion over the next few months."

In April 1995, while in Changsha with a team, the director phoned David's hotel and told him today was the day when they would visit the Ministry of Civil Affairs. David had been preparing for such a meeting, but its abrupt timing came as a surprise.

Director Zhou picked up David and Carmen Tyler, who had been involved right from ICC's establishment. A youthful looking twenty-four, David needed someone older to provide the gravitas he felt he lacked.

In the car, he said to Carmen: "If this meeting goes well, the door opens. If not, the door is shut."

With trepidation, they arrived at the Ministry of Civil Affairs, climbed the few steps to the lobby, then a further three flights and were led slightly breathless into a room to face the Director of Social Welfare for Changsha City, and his deputy. "I remember the unease as I faced these two unemotional government officials who, it seemed, had no desire to be wasting their time speaking to me."

Speaking in Chinese, David shared his vision for a long-term partnership between ICC and the Changsha No. 1 Welfare Centre. After months of planning, David and his team had come up with a proposal that they hoped the officials would agree to. In the past two years, they had never openly criticized the Chinese welfare system and they weren't about to now. Instead they pitched the idea of establishing China's first joint venture of a model welfare centre.

Focusing on the officials' sense of pride, he told them what he believed they wanted to hear. The model centre would be a place where effective rehabilitation would be used to give children with disabilities a chance to achieve their fullest potential. The Changsha Welfare Centre's standards would attract recognition from all over the country. People would come and see a professional system of care for disabled children as well as a welfare centre staff training centre that taught leadership in paediatric care, paediatric occupational and physical therapy, and child development and psychology.

David recalls:

My presentation that day was a reflection on what
we wanted to achieve in Changsha but, for me, it was
deeper. It was a sense that God wanted to create a
home, a family, a place of safety and nurture for these
vulnerable children whom He loved. I knew that if
God raised up the right people, ICC would bring them
together to invest their skills, experience, passion, and
love into making the dreams of this God-centred family
become a reality that would shine in China. For the
government, the chance to be part of something like this
was irresistible.

Throughout his presentation, the government officials showed
no sign of encouragement. They remained stony-faced and
unresponsive. At one point, David felt intimidated enough to lean
over to Carmen to whisper in English, "Please pray!" The meeting
was going badly – and this was the make-or-break meeting.

David sank back into his chair knowing that whatever
happened next was in God's hands. Unexpectedly the two officials
brightened and smiled. David and Carmen were taken aback.
"We have been watching you. We have been looking at what you
do, how you do it, and we appreciate what you have been doing
for these children." They went on to say that they were open to
working with ICC in the long term and that the details would be
worked out. The two officials then stood up, forcing David and
Carmen to rise; they shook hands warmly and motioned toward
the door.

On the way back to the welfare centre David and Carmen
couldn't believe what had happened. "I sat in the car feeling
completely spent. We knew that somehow God had performed
a miracle in the hearts of these two men." They couldn't wait to

tell the team, but that would come later. As they pulled into the welfare centre gateway, Director Zhou said to the driver, "Stop here!" He told David to get out and follow him and he disappeared around a corner near the entrance of the compound.

David had no idea what was going on but he chased the director around the side of the welfare centre building to be faced with a derelict, dirty one-storey building. Pointing to it, Director Zhou proudly announced, "This is your building."

David stared at this crumbling ruin wondering how they could make anything of it. He could see holes in the ancient ceramic tiles where water would pour in during the rainy season. The windows were broken, and the walls were blackened and dirty. They climbed over the rubble and ducked their heads as they entered the building. The floors were unsealed, and the walls were made of brick and mud plaster. There was an overwhelming stench from the toilets. It even made the existing conditions that the children were living in look good. It was tough to imagine anything for this place other than demolition. David walked across the rubble back into the daylight. Then he turned round to look again. He saw something new:

Superimposed on the ruin was another image – one of beauty. A roof repaired with new tiles, walls smooth and painted, the windows weren't broken, and there was grass where the rubble had been. I could imagine the sound of children playing, running, and skipping, joy and laughter bursting forth. In that moment I knew God was giving me a vision of what He would do in that place. He would repair the broken walls of that building, and He would also repair the broken lives of the children that lived there.

Director Zhou turned and said, "What do you think?" David was already smiling, "It's perfect!" The ruin in which the coal was stored had a diamond within.

The coal store

The next day, as he stood looking at the building, David whispered a prayer and three letters dropped into his mind: MMM – Mobile Mission Maintenance. During his very first few homesick days in Hong Kong at High Rock where he had completed his YWAM programme three years previously, David had met an older Australian couple who had been kind to him.

They had shared that their work was to serve by doing building and maintenance projects for other NGOs, but he didn't know much else about them. He found a contact address and wrote a letter to them (there were no emails at that time) about this dilapidated building in the middle of China, and the vision he had to see it restored and redeemed. A couple of weeks later he got a reply to say that one of MMM's leaders called Graham Young was going to be in Hong Kong shortly and he would come to Changsha to have a look at the building.

A month later, David and Graham walked together into the welfare centre. David nervously knew that what he was about to show Graham would challenge even those with the strongest of faith. Enthusiastically he pointed to the ruinous structure and announced, "This is it!" His enthusiasm wavered as he saw the look of shock on his new friend's face. "I mumbled something about the vision of children with care and healing, playing in a fully restored building."

When Graham realized David was serious, he said: "Leave me alone for a while," and he turned back to look at the building. For the next two days his experienced eyes cast around a building that had stored coal, acted as a repair shop for taxis, and was now a rubbish dump. He saw dirt floors, no bathrooms, dangerous wiring, leaking pipes, broken walls, serious structural issues, and grounds outside that were covered with industrial debris. But Graham could also imagine what the ruin would look like fixed up. He took measurements and conducted a feasibility assessment.

Two days after that, Graham sat David down. "I felt nervous because even I could see that the building was ripe for demolition." The complexities of Graham's technical discussion faded into the words "We can do this" and at that moment David's vision came alive. "I saw that not only would God transform the lives of children abandoned because of their disabilities, but that the vision would catch fire in people's hearts."

And the first hearts were those of the plumbers, carpenters, tilers, roofers, and decorators who over the next year would leave their families for weeks at a time so that some of China's most vulnerable children could have a place to call home.

Lyndel

Graham Young returned to Australia to recruit those workers. His daughter Lyndel remembered how pumped up he was by the experience. "I remember Dad was so excited – and he doesn't usually get that excited! He had lots of photos and stories and was keen to introduce ICC to me. I thought I'd like to check this out for myself."

China was not a complete unknown to Lyndel. Graham and his wife Elizabeth had also been based in Hong Kong in High Rock in the 1980s and 90s and she had actually visited Changsha in 1992, well before ICC had made their first unplanned trip.

Lyndel's first trip had been a stark contrast to modern, big-city Hong Kong. Most of the roads in Changsha were made of dirt and China was drab and grey. People in the street wore the old Mao jacket or padded duvets, in lifeless colours. Goods were exchanged in coins and what notes were used were worn, battered, and dirty. Foreigners were not supposed to use them and had to make do with Foreign Exchange Certificates, which were exchanged for foreign currency at a much inferior rate. Speakers broadcast loud propaganda throughout the day, especially in the Hunan University area, where they were staying. They were told not to talk about Christianity while they were there, even privately inside apartments.

She thought that she might have the kind of background needed in the field for an orphanage of disabled children. She had seven years' experience as an occupational therapist and although much of this had been with adults, it was still relevant.

Lyndel had never thought of working for an NGO, even though Graham had been involved in building facilities for missions most of Lyndel's life. As a child she had been exposed to missionaries, as they had often come through her house but she had always thought, "Oh, I'd never want to do that!" To her, even as a child, they had all looked dowdy and... well... a bit out of touch with reality.

China seemed interesting and the project sounded enticing. Lyndel and her husband Shane, both not yet thirty, applied to go on one of the first regular teams in late 1995. David Gotts, the young man with the vision that had inspired Graham, was organizing and leading the team. Gertrud Schweizer had joined the April 1995 team from Switzerland. "I expected the leader to be in their forties with greying hair, but here was this... schoolboy!" Her shock soon dissipated. "He was so much part of the team, no sense of him being in authority. He was a lovely person and had such a vision and passion for the work. He was more than capable of doing the job."

David talked them through his ambition in the wet, grey, cloudy, wintry weather of Changsha as they circled the derelict building. Gertrud said, "While God moved my heart, it was Dave that inspired me." It was also uncomfortable as he challenged each one by asking, "Where do you fit in? What are you going to do about it?"

Lyndel wanted to accept David's challenge. "Initially China was shocking but there was also a deep fascination and excitement because it was so different to anything in Australia."

At the end of the visit, Lyndel, Shane, and on the other side of the world Gertrud, felt an urgent pull to go back. The next eighteen months were spent talking through the idea with family and friends, giving notice at their jobs, raising financial support, and then applying to go into China full time.

Gertrud spoke for all of them. "If you are called to something you just fit in, despite the stresses. There were many frustrations throughout the language learning and the 'This is China' times – but never any regrets." In fact, she said, "We were attracted to this group of young people from many parts of the world with a passion to start something new that would benefit abandoned and disabled children."

CHAPTER 7

China's Oasis

For Harry and Tina Hoffmann even to hear about ICC when they were so far away in Berlin was remarkable. It so happened that Ross Paterson's CCSM had an office in Potsdam nearby, but this German-Austrian couple had been interested in China long before then.

Tina had a calling to go to China from the age of thirteen, but that had dimmed with marriage and children. Now in his late twenties, Harry had a newly minted Master's degree in Chinese Studies and was again lighting that candle.

Then, on cue, they were struck by a 1995 BBC documentary about the "Dying Rooms", and a documentary by the Amity Foundation highlighting the plight of abandoned children in China. With CCSM's endorsement, the Hoffmanns packed up their two kids and bought a one-way trip to Taiwan, arriving on 8 January 1996.

Meanwhile it was becoming obvious that the two Daves needed to relocate from Taiwan to Hong Kong to be closer to the work. David was conscious of the need to build a team of people that could live on the ground in Changsha to realize the vision. "I knew how my time with YWAM had shaped my view of how God wanted me to work in a foreign land so, working with CCSM, David Clarkson and I began to formulate a curriculum that could equip and train people for long-term service in China."

The small team who were to work alongside David to launch ICC in Changsha made final preparations for their move to the city. Two nurses, Gertrud Schweizer and Lily Oh, a Mandarin-speaking Malaysian-Chinese lady from the UK; and Andrew and Angela Walker, a retired teacher and nurse from the UK, had applied. Tim and Carmen Tyler, who had served for many years in Taiwan, had been marked as the leaders of the team within China but were recalled to the US at short notice. Plans to open a school in Taipei were shelved in favour of ICC relocating to Hong Kong to be closer to the work. Harry and Tina were then asked if they would work in China instead of Taiwan as part of an initial team of six. They were asked to replace the Tylers – temporarily.

Their first nights were spent in the (by now) infamous Liu Fang Hotel – the hotel that David's first Changsha team had found; then (as now) cheap and not particularly cheerful.

Harry was shocked by the conditions that the children lived in:

As you came into the welfare centre, the first room
on the right was a reception room full of potty chairs.
The next looked like a cattle shed, just a bare dark
and grey concrete room, so full of cots that you could
hardly move between them. Many of the children of
the future ICC were in that room, like Wang Gui and
Wang Hua, who lay next to each other communicating
with breaths and sounds. The humidity was so high that
water was dripping down the walls and onto the floor.
Occasionally you'd see the head or tail of one of the
massive rats running around in the drains.

The two Daves established the Hong Kong office to organize the support for the field team. "It was fantastically busy. Harry and Tina were settling into their roles as team leaders, the team were developing an operational platform for the new children's centre, and I was preparing for the large contingent of Aussie workers coming to renovate the building."

Things start to come together

In the midst of supporting the team and managing relations with the government, David also keenly felt the need for the money required to pay for the building supplies and fit out the building. The need to pray for provision had never been so great. God was providing people – team members and those that would renovate the building. Now David needed God to miraculously provide the money.

David's fundraising trips had begun to take him all over the world: Australia, the UK, Hong Kong, and to North America. The more he met people and spoke with churches, the more his infectious, boyish enthusiasm captivated them, and the more they invited him to come and speak about the work.

His exciting descriptions about working in China brought in much-needed funds – never too much, but just enough to break even. More importantly, word of mouth spread about this exciting project coming to life in China and this helped the recruitment effort. "I felt humbled by the response of those that heard of the needs of China's abandoned and disabled children. After twenty or thirty minutes of speaking I would be inundated by those who wanted to get involved in some way."

David was also a great delegator, spotting talent in people who could do a job even when they had not thought of it themselves. He realized the need to empower those around him so that he was not overwhelmed. Despite his new leadership role, David welcomed others taking on responsibility. "I had to rely on others to take on tasks that they had never done before. There was no one else. I lost count of the times someone in ICC would take on a job knowing that only God could equip those called."

Before returning to Hong Kong from Changsha, David asked Harry if he would take on full responsibility for the Oasis House project and also for the growing team. He knew that he was asking a lot of Harry and his family. So, less than six months after leaving Berlin, still in their twenties with two small children, Harry and Tina were now responsible for a permanent team based in the Changsha Welfare Centre. They were learning fast about the shifting nature of events in China.

Harry was leading the whole of ICC's work in China, including running the office, balancing the books, dealing with foreign visitors, organizing the renovations, translating, buying construction equipment, making decisions as an ICC board director, and being the point man for the Civil Affairs Bureau and the welfare centre. His previous job had been as an accountant's bookkeeper to raise money for his university Chinese studies. "This is China, Harry."

There was no time to take stock – they were fully immersed. The leadership was very young – David Gotts was five years younger than Harry and Tina. David said, "None of us knew that we were seemingly attempting the impossible. We had too much to do. We were too inexperienced, and we lived with the knowledge that for some of the children, we weren't moving quickly enough."

Harry remembers, "We were the first ones; it was all pioneering work." There was a thick Overseas Missionary Fellowship handbook on working in China that had been written with the benefit of over 100 years of mission experience. In their enthusiasm they dismissed it. "There was no need for a handbook. We were faith driven. God had called us and would lead us." They remembered with shock being told that a well-established missionary organization recommended putting children into boarding school before coming to China so that they would not be a distraction.

Their own pre-school children were very happy making

friends with the children in the welfare centre where they went every day with their mum and dad. As Tina said, "My daughter never saw the kids as being handicapped or even Chinese – she said that they were her friends like any other children."

Building the vision

The welfare centre provided accommodation by moving the Family Planning Office out and renovating a floor to provide four flats for the permanent team members – the Walkers, Gertrud, Lily Oh, and the Hoffmann family.

Gertrud remembers living on mattresses and boxes until furniture was made. They didn't have much electricity and when they did it was only enough for a light bulb or an electric fan. It was frustrating if the water stopped when they were standing in the shower covered in soap. They quickly learned to store water for such occasions.

It was hard to cope with the extreme heat and dampness of summer – it made everyone feel tired and dizzy – and wonderful to find a room with air-conditioning. During the first winter even Gertrud from Switzerland had to learn how to keep warm. "Back in 1996, no house, no shop, no bus, or car was heated. It was cold just everywhere." They did not have enough warm clothes. "The local employees gave me warm underwear and two ladies knitted woollen leggings for me. No shop existed to buy clothes in Western sizes. This has changed a lot over the years."

Later visitors had a much easier introduction, for in 1998 foreigners were permitted to rent furnished flats anywhere in the city, electric fan heaters were more common, and household items could be handed down to newcomers. The welfare centre gave some support but their real interest was in ICC's work and money.

Sixty Australian tradesmen recruited by Graham – plumbers, bricklayers, painters, carpenters, electricians, engineers, and decorators – descended in the spring of 1996. They took holiday from their regular jobs and paid their own costs to come to China to work their magical skills on an old coal store for the children.

While they were doing that, Gertrud spent five months in the language school in Changsha (on top of four months' learning in Taiwan) but was in the orphanage three times a week. "Soon I knew each single child by name and got to know their individual personality and condition."

Gertrud had wanted to be a missionary from childhood but she was over thirty by the time she read the biography of CIM's founder, Hudson Taylor. "China was very much on my heart. But I did not know how to get involved."

She then read Ross Paterson's book, *Heartcry for China*.[5] "Through this book I learned a lot about CCSM and that there was a need for an orphanage." That led to her joining the April 1995 ICC team, led by Crystal Kelleher and David Gotts.

This was the team that had been given the coal store and was when David had spoken about his idea to put a permanent ICC team into the orphanage. "I felt called to that place. I have always had a heart for children with disabilities. Hearing about ICC's work was the door to China opening for me." For ICC to attract Gertrud as a founder volunteer who was a trained nurse and social worker with twenty years' experience was a real blessing.

Gertrud was quickly able to connect with children with disabilities. "I longed to spend time with them in the orphanage. While I was there time was so short that it seemed like a drop of water on a hot stone. Sometimes I asked myself, 'What can I accomplish on my own to care for sixty children with disabilities?'"

She was dismayed at the neglect shown to children kept on potty chairs throughout the day and sensed the urgent need to get children placed in a newer centre. The team renamed the colloquially named "Potty-chair Room" to "The Room of Hope".

They lived over the shop, working twelve-hour days, seven days a week, and often had to attend emergencies in the small hours.

Meanwhile, David, Harry, and especially Crystal (by now a key member of the permanent team), helped Graham scour the markets for building materials as the team gutted and transformed the building. Harry's specialist Chinese vocabulary for building materials expanded dramatically. "We spent long days weaving our way across the city sourcing steel beams, pipes, wires, windows, doors, tiles, toilets, washbasins, bathtubs, planks, cables, paint, and paintbrushes. The list was never ending. It all had to be ready for when the team arrived so that we could maximize their time and get the renovations completed."

The MMM teams constructed the building to high Australian building standards. As a first in Changsha, wheelchair access was incorporated from the beginning and the premises were designed to avoid accidental injury. It was an incredible task to transform a shell, in less than a year, into a large villa with bedrooms, bathrooms, offices, classrooms, therapy rooms, and a medical clinic – but they did.

Where MMM didn't manage to complete something, the local team provided the finishing touches. Two Dutch couples, Martin and Margreet Peschar and Sylvia and Fritz Vander Puten, brought their children to Changsha for a time to help renovate the building.[6] The interiors were finished with the help of a Chinese builder. Gertrud found a skill she never knew she had: "I realized a dream from my childhood into a reality. I discovered that I am gifted in design! I enjoyed designing furniture for the building. As a child, I had daydreamed about building an orphanage, down to each single detail."

She and Tina began to fit out the inside of the house with the goal of turning the ruin into a home. They chose chairs, desks, kitchen equipment, curtains, and bedding, and designed the space so that each child would have their own bed and storage cupboard. They knew that this would be the first time the children would have owned personal items and to stimulate their sense of individuality, each bed and space had a sticker to show who it belonged to.

As they worked, the ruin came to life. The building would allow them to move children from a dank, dirty, and impersonal institution to a bright and loving, personal home. Together they established a 24/7 institution, with capacity for twenty children and staff to provide the round-the-clock care.

A place to call home

David remembers when the grass for the garden was laid and in the middle of the grey and dusty city of Changsha, a special little green space emerged. Tina designed a playground with a sandpit, a hill for the kids to roll down, a board with different textures to explore, a wooden train to sit in, a path around the grass as a road for tricycles, and a swing especially designed to secure a child with a disability who would sit or lie in a net held open by a stainless steel ring.

"I felt very privileged. I had seen God's vision become a reality." A small group stood in the garden praying for a name for this now lovely building and one of the team members read out a passage from Isaiah 41 (verses 17–20):

> The poor and needy search for water, but there is none;
> their tongues are parched with thirst. But I the Lord
> will answer them... I will make rivers flow on barren
> heights, and springs within the valleys. I will turn the
> desert into pools of water, and the parched ground into
> springs. ... I will set junipers in the wasteland, the fir
> and the cypress together, so that people may see and
> know... that the hand of the Lord has done this.

The coal store had been transformed and they believed the same transformation would soon take place in the children's lives. It was named Oasis House.

The verses became the heart of the work of Oasis House, and it marked the start of ICC's permanent presence in China. It was now July 1996 and the long-term ICC residential team in Changsha was growing. They were now able to build sustainable relationships with the children in the welfare centre and conduct proper needs assessments.

A strong team from all over the world had collaborated and accomplished the impossible in a very short time. Led on the ground by people like Graham, Gertrud, the Hoffmanns, Lily, and the Walkers, they innovated, experimented, and established – helped by a multitude of people from outside China who freely gave of their time and money. When David thought about it, the finished project may have been slightly different from what he had envisaged, but it had turned out exactly as it was meant to be.

Opening the Oasis

Harry and Tina Hoffmann kept one eye on their daughters aged two and three who were playing with the ICC kids at the opening ceremony at Oasis House. The 10 January 1997 was cloudy, with the cold and airborne coal dust making it difficult to breathe. It should have been a celebration of a job completed but Tina felt as if the day were an anti-climax and had a heavy heart.

The team had worked hard to get Oasis House ready. They had planned an opening ceremony because David had recognized how critical it was to honour the partnership with the government for providing the basis for ICC's model of care for disabled children.

They invited the orphanage directors and the Changsha city social welfare officials to share the pride of the opening. They had a stroke of luck. The very same weekend, the National Civil Affairs Conference was due to be held in Changsha. All the provincial representatives for civil affairs from across China would be in the city, including the national Minister for Social Welfare. So they sent him an invitation to open Oasis House – and were thrilled when he accepted.

The opening ceremony went very smoothly. The Minister for Social Welfare, Terry Phillips (ICC's board chairman), and Jean Mclellan each planted a tree outside Oasis House. The trees symbolized how Oasis House would break new ground and enable new life to grow. Jean's tree immediately tilted to one side, to the accompaniment of uproarious laughter.

David and the ICC team could not believe that God had orchestrated the timing so perfectly that the minister from Beijing would be opening Oasis House – the first non-government residential centre for disabled children in China. Receiving this kind of acknowledgment from the government was vitally important. ICC's long-term work would only be successful if they could do it in partnership with the authorities, setting an example, and showing what could be done.

He knew that ICC had to become a respected organization with a good image, and the opening of Oasis House brought them a reputation and a credibility that otherwise would have been hard to achieve. He felt deeply thankful for God's leading and provision. A few months later, when they launched the social welfare training programme, they were able to use this reputation and train staff and directors from orphanages across Hunan Province, and then across China.

The opening of Oasis House would not change the whole of China, but he was encouraged that they were moving forwards toward the vision of seeing abandoned and disabled children being valued and respected in their country. The team believed that Oasis House would be "a town built on a hill [that] cannot be hidden" and that light would shine out from a dark place (Matthew 5:14).

Tina remembers the day of celebration being one of her hardest days. The parody was that the walls of the government welfare centre had been newly plastered for the visit of the minister and it crumbled off two weeks later. "It was as if heaven and earth came crashing together. It was not a day of celebration but a burden, a very strong fight." The last year had been one of constantly managing intensive deadlines, and despite the success of the project she felt that their physical, mental, and spiritual needs were getting left behind, leaving them vulnerable.

David remembers the day with joy – but the evening with sadness. When he returned home after the celebratory banquet with the government officials, he discovered that a key team member and a close friend, Fred,[7] had been lying to him. He had suspected that things were not good for a while, as his friend had begun to take a dangerous path.

The cloud that David had been walking upon all day dissolved beneath his feet as long meetings continued into the night. The nature of life in full-time ministry in a foreign country is often that the highest highs are followed by the lowest lows.

CHAPTER 8

From Neglect to Family

T he most emotional job of all was yet to come. Harry explained, "It was traumatic deciding which kids to take into Oasis House. The process took months. Gertrud had a long list, which we painstakingly refined. Even as we did that, we found it almost impossible to decide."

The demand was so great that they could never meet the needs of all the children. David worried about it. "Making the decision between bringing children into Oasis House and leaving them in the welfare centre was the difference between life and death." This put the team under enormous pressure. "If you choose this child you have to leave that child, and we knew that inevitably meant suffering and often death."

The team were dealing with tragic human conditions. Nearly all the children had been abandoned by their parents because of their disabilities; many had faced terrible abuse and neglect, leaving them frail and weakened. Children could sicken and die in front of their eyes and in their arms, leaving them feeling helpless and impotent. The welfare centre staff didn't seem to care and operated on an alien set of values, which the team understood in context, but that made it no less painful.

After a long process, the children selected were of differing ages and had a broad range of disabilities. They picked those whom they thought they could help most in the shortest period of time. Gertrud wanted to take them all: "I was crying and hurting for these children. To me it was a tragedy without end." Each child had their own story, and their own need for love and care.

They decided that the first children to move into Oasis House would be a group of eight boys, but in early January 1997, they welcomed eight boys and a girl to their new home.

The team had met Wang Gui and Wang Hua, a boy and a girl then four years of age, on their first short-term team trip to Changsha in 1994. David remembers seeing them for the first time, lying twisted awkwardly on wooden pallets. They were unable to move and collected pressure sores on their bodies. Wang Gui was paralysed from the waist down with spina bifida and Wang Hua had cerebral palsy.

Both children were emotionally distant but the team noticed they had a very special relationship with each other. They were non-verbal, technically, but communicated with each other in a series of sounds as if it were their own language. They seemed to sustain one another and drew strength from their closeness. The two children were actually keeping each other alive. The team were touched by this tender connection and David paid special attention to them each time he visited. He prayed each time he left Changsha that both would still be around the next time he returned.

During one team visit there was an outbreak of chicken pox at the welfare centre. Twelve children died as they developed blisters in their throats and were unable to eat. David walked in one day and saw that Wang Gui was on the edge of death. He had stopped eating and was withered and emaciated. In those days, the welfare centre rarely sent children to hospital, so David and the team sat with him for days, patiently dripping liquid into his mouth through a medicine dropper to keep him hydrated, and talking to him to keep him engaged.

With the love of the team and lots of prayer Wang Gui survived and he was selected as one of the eight boys who would be in the initial intake at Oasis House. "Then we realized that if we took Wang Gui and left Wang Hua in the welfare centre, she would lose her will to live." They had been together for so long in such a hopeless place that they had built up a resilience to survive together. If Wang Gui were to be left on his own, Wang Hua would assume he had died, without realizing that Wang Gui had gone somewhere better. "So we had to take Wang Hua too – they had helped each other to cling to life for so long that they both deserved to be given a chance of life through Oasis House."

Another boy chosen was Li Shi, who had been five when the team first found him in the Changsha Welfare Centre. His father had died and his mother couldn't look after him. His early childhood had been happy and although he was now surrounded by hopelessness and death, his spirit still shone. He had cerebral palsy, walking was a challenge, and his speech was unclear, but the team loved him. Despite his circumstances, Li Shi's heart and spirit remained hopeful, and a few months later he would move into his new home, with his new family, in Oasis House.

One evening after dinner, David returned to the welfare centre, something he didn't normally do. He was feeling overwhelmed about the challenges; the need was so huge. "All I could offer at that moment was to walk outside and pray for the children lying helplessly in their cribs."

He ran into Li Shi, who said, "*Ni lai zuo shenme?* What are you doing here?" David explained that he was asking God to come and help each of the children. Then out of the blue he found himself saying, "Li Shi, do you think you could pray for me?" Li Shi put his hand on his shoulder and quietly prayed the most wonderful prayer. Although his speech was slurred and his language was hard to understand, David sensed the heart of this tender boy and, encouraged, he knew that God was answering Li Shi's prayer.

Zheng Quan had cerebral palsy of a type that made him very floppy, with uncontrolled movements, but he was very interactive with a beautiful smile. He worked his way into Lyndel's heart during her first visit to the Changsha Welfare Centre. He lacked control of his arms and legs, so Lyndel, bringing all her therapy skills to bear, worked with him each day for two weeks to help build up strength in his body.

Gertrud noticed that while Zheng Quan's coordination was poor he could still move quickly. One day he found a ping-pong ball and quick as a flash popped it into his mouth. Due to his lack of control, he could do nothing to expel the ball, and worse, his instinct was to swallow.

Gertrud and Angela tried to remove the ball but Gertrud saw with horror that "while we watched, he started to suffocate".

David was crossing the courtyard for lunch when he heard the cries. Zheng Quan lay blue and unconscious, but David was able to creep one of his long fingers into Zheng Quan's throat, knowing that it was imperative for the ball not to be pushed. Somehow his crooked finger slid behind the ball and it popped out. Gertrud recalls, "They were traumatic seconds for all of us... and they seemed to last an eternity. We are so grateful that Zheng Quan's life was saved and that he was no worse for wear."

The children reach home

Chen Shi was excited as Harry carried him across the yard to Oasis House. He thought, "It feels like I'm going to heaven!" Until he was thirteen, Chen Shi had seldom been outside the welfare centre. The few times he had been were when ICC team members introduced him to the outside world through visits to the park, or to buy an ice-cream at the corner shop. He could only imagine what was in the noise and bustle of the streets over the wall. He never went to school, though he was taught to write his name and to do some basic arithmetic.

He knew why he was in the welfare centre. "I was told that I came to the orphanage as a tiny baby." His parents abandoned him seeing that he was born with a dislocated spine and was paralysed from the waist down. In those days, this made him an outcast in Chinese society, despite being a beautiful and intelligent boy.

Life in the orphanage was very hard. His abiding memory is one of hunger. "Just one bowl between five or six kids," he recalls in English, "and when it was gone, no more." Summer was very hot; the winter was very cold: "clothes not enough". His body always felt weak. Death was ever present with a weekly turnover of children, often his friends. They were constantly sick and no one slept well because of the noise, or the bugs that infested their cotton quilts.

He was wary of the *ayis*, or carers, in those days. "They had little love, you know; they spoke strongly, and when they were angry they hit the kids." Chen Shi was OK; he could speak well and feed himself. In fact, he became a favourite because he could help the *ayis*. He had no wheelchair so he used an old wooden chair, shifting his body to scrape along the floor. Mostly, he just crawled at high speed – he was athletic and fast.

Before ICC had come to Changsha, an American visitor to the welfare centre had seen the eight-year old Chen Shi struggling to be mobile. The next time the American visited, he brought him a local second-hand wheelchair. It lasted Chen Shi a couple of years but when it broke there was nobody to repair it and Chen Shi had to use the old wooden chair once more.

It was exciting when ICC began coming to the welfare centre. "I was always amazed that David could speak Chinese so well!" Soon, Chinese volunteers, often from the local church, heard of the children and came to spend time entertaining them. "I loved the stories that they told." Chen Shi began to sense God's love in the way that both the local and foreign volunteers cared for them.

It took a year to restore Oasis House and during that time Chen Shi "loved playing with the Australian guys. Oh such fun!" He was an older boy, mobile and very chirpy, and he befriended the Australian workers brought in by David from Mobile Mission Maintenance. While they couldn't speak each other's language, it didn't stop them communicating, and Chen Shi's English improved. He was known by his nickname Shi Tou (石头), meaning Rock, although the volunteers gave him an English name, John. He now calls himself Johnny.

Chen Shi also became friends with the children of the volunteers, who spoke native Chinese learned in the local school. The Hoffmanns and their children provided him with a family role model. "They were cool. I loved them!"

He was the eldest of the first eight children moved to Oasis House. "It was the beginning of my second life, my new life. I can tell you what it was like – everything was new, like a new baby. I had my own bed. So soft, ah! I had my own dish and for the first time I used a knife and fork and had my own chopsticks! I had lots of toys – there was a whole room of toys. Wah! Everything, lots of toys."

And outside there was a playground "like Disney! I liked the grass; it was green and cool; and they had a little sandpit. Just crazy. I like." The helpers were very different too. "Nice and I could feel love. I could feel that this is love."

The daily fight for survival was over. He loved being part of a family that cared for each other and played and worshipped together. Christmas was a favourite time, whether it was decorating the house, putting on a show, singing carols, or exchanging gifts and food. And he enthusiastically celebrated Chinese New Year with his Oasis House brothers and sisters. It was now a great opportunity to eat and hang out together, just like any other Chinese family.

Child development

The first eight children moved into the Jasper Room. Gertrud recorded: "It is so amazing to watch how they have blossomed in such a short time." Liu Guang, who had been very depressed, started to smile and express joy with his whole body. "Wang Gui and Wang Hua enjoyed being picked up and held – whereas before they had flinched when approached." They were now seven years old but had never spoken; yet now they began to smile and form words, and picked up toys, passing them back and forth to each other.

The children began to develop at their own pace. Chen Shi had access to a doctor that ICC employed and received long-awaited medical attention for his paralysis. He began to receive regular physical therapy to strengthen his limbs. It wasn't long before a sponsor bought him a new wheelchair, giving him the kind of mobility and freedom that he craved.

Not only did his physical development improve, but Chen Shi exhibited a keen intelligence and quickly overtook every student in the Oasis House school, so much so that within two years he was able to attend a mainstream school, outside the welfare centre compound.

David had found it a real battle to get the local schools to accept Chen Shi. "We would approach them and ask whether they would accept children from Oasis House. As soon as the principal of the school heard of any disability they would simply refuse." Chinese law actually compelled state schools to accept students with disabilities, but as they knew, in China the reality is often different. One school finally agreed to take Chen Shi, while at the same time expressing a desire for a new computer, a small price to pay for free tuition. "Despite this, any modifications to help Chen Shi were rebuffed, leaving him to navigate flights of stairs. But Chen Shi showed a determination that he was unwilling to give up."

Chen Shi was determined but it was still hard. He had no friends and talked to no classmates. He was much older – they were six or seven years old; he was now thirteen. There were too many questions like, "Why do you sit in a chair? Why are you like that?" He pushed himself into quiet study, as he could do nothing else.

He loved being in ICC but "outside, no way. When I first walked outside on the street, my eyes… I always looked down. I was afraid of people watching me. I couldn't watch their eyes. I feel it's bad that they think I'm different."

One day, Lucy Chua from Singapore, who served ICC for sixteen years from 2000, told him, "Hey, Chen Shi, you know, you shouldn't fear other people watching you. You are a star. People watch you, so you should be happy. They look at a movie star – lots of people watch you! Think about it and try to change."

But it was hard to do, with all the effort of wheeling himself to school and the embarrassment of having a local ICC staff member come to the school to carry him up and down the stairs to class.

One day one of the foreign volunteers encouraged him. "You need to change from your heart. Smile at yourself and smile at people. When you smile, people will smile back to you. So I tried again. When I walked the road, I looked up into their eyes and tried to smile. YES! It was working. People see you smile and they smile back. Every day I would look and smile at people." Shopkeepers and passers-by already knew of him as he wheeled to school every day and they began to say hello to him like a friend.

"At school, I smiled to make friends; I surprised myself as I talked and played with everyone. Things had really changed and so had I. The solution to the problem was in my heart and mind… and my smile."

Taking stock

Harry recalls that in time they were able to accommodate even more children within Oasis House. "We turned a staff room into a bedroom and we were able to take four more kids. Then we looked at developing the winter coal room for storage, but when we cleared it out we thought, 'We can't use it as storage – this room is too big!'" Gertrud called it the Diamond Room and it became home for nine more children, pushing the final number up to forty-three.

The improved nutrition provided by the Oasis House kitchens meant that the children began to grow healthier and their development accelerated. The children gradually grew secure in the knowledge that breakfast would be followed by lunch and dinner, rather than having to live with the previous uncertainty. Of course, every dish at every meal was spiked with Hunan's intense chilli. Sue Munday, a newly arrived occupational therapist, recalls that when the ICC team used to eat in Oasis House, the kitchen staff quietly gave the foreigners food without the chilli overload so loved by the hot-blooded Hunanese.

Even David never quite got used to the spiciness of the food. "I loved the food in Changsha but shrank when I saw the children loading on the chilli in a way that caused me to melt. The children laughed at the watering eyes of the foreign volunteers." Hunan food is otherwise excellent and even today David will sneak out to hunt down a cheap and delicious street breakfast.

They hired more local staff to be caregivers and teachers for the increased numbers of children, and established a routine of education, therapy, and life-skills classes. Selma van der Meulen from Holland joined the team. Angela Walker and Lily Oh turned an old storeroom into a clinic that met the complex medical needs of the children. Together, staff and children created a sense of family. Children who had never had consistent connections with adults were now spoken to by the same caregivers daily, and they came to understand this was their home.

Gertrud recalled that the move to Oasis House caused a dramatic change in the children: "In order for everyone to get to know the incoming children, their pictures were placed up on a notice board with their name and history. A few months later, a volunteer photographed the children again. It was only when they put the new and old next to each other that we realized how much the children had flourished – even before they had any therapy or special treatment. The children blossomed because they were loved, respected, and treated as individuals."

CHAPTER 9

This is China: A Mission Journey

ICC had decided to run a mission training school like the one David had attended at High Rock just a few years earlier. There was a century and a half of tradition in the training of missionaries dating back to the early days of the CIM itself. "I had experienced first-hand how God had used my YWAM training to equip me to start the work of ICC. I wanted that to be shared by those willing to trust God with me as we stumbled along the road."

David felt that the training and his recent experiences with ICC had shown him that God had opened a door and was establishing a work. Bringing those who wished to serve together for a period of time was a way of seeing how individuals could bond personally and spiritually, and provide a sense of how they would cope living in a different culture.

"This last aspect was critical. From my first day with YWAM I had been told that more people returned from overseas service because of a breakdown in relationships between team members than for any other reason. If we could unite in a shared sense of purpose and identity around the belief that God wanted to use us in China, it would form a foundation that could withstand the challenges ahead."

David wanted ICC to be a place where anyone who felt called could come with willing hearts and skills, but he was also alert to the fact that some volunteers had to deal with personal issues before they came to China. "You could not escape something just by coming to China, because those issues were likely to be amplified by the stresses of the field."

On the other hand, he also recalled that one of China's most renowned missionaries was Gladys Aylward, who had made her own way to China having been deemed unsuitable to serve overseas by the CIM itself.[8] The mission training school was a great way for people to bond in a less stressful environment.

The two Daves had a shared vision of China training but they were beginning to have diverging interests. David's focus was still on abandoned and disabled children. David Clarkson was by now looking at a broader mission with an emphasis on training. The goal was the same: to train people to serve the Chinese in the most effective way.

So instead of going into China, at the end of 1996 Lyndel and Shane found themselves spending four months at the Lutheran Training College at Dao Fung Shan in Hong Kong. It is a beautiful and peaceful location set on the hill well above Shatin, amidst an aromatic section of pine forest. Despite the peaceful surroundings, they still hankered after the excitement of the field.

Dave Clarkson ran the course with Terry and Rose Phillips, and visiting speakers such as Jackie Pullinger, Jean Mclellan, Harry Hoffmann, and David himself came to add their experiences. Dawn Gage was asked to attend the course even though she was already a highly experienced NGO professional and had indeed first discovered the terrible circumstances of China's abandoned children a few years earlier. She was looking to partner with ICC in developing the Living Stones Village Orphanage back in Nanning, Guangxi Province.

They were given wide-ranging lectures covering discipleship, personality profiling, and how to get on culturally in the field.

They also went to see ICC's work first-hand, including attending the Oasis House opening ceremony.

Despite the commitment of leaving their careers and friends behind in faith, there was no word from ICC throughout the course that Lyndel and Shane had been accepted. It crossed their minds that it might not happen. Lyndel remembered thinking ICC's administration was pretty disorganized. "Taking that into account, it was a big ask to leave our family, friends and career," admitted Lyndel, but one to which they were still committed.

Only at the very end of the course did they hear that ICC needed them… Now! "We were given six weeks to pack up in Australia with the intention of moving to Changsha in the second half of 1997." They had begun to realize that ICC was just a baby in organizational terms and everybody was still at the start of the journey – but it still seemed chaotic.

Just as they had packed for China, a request came from David. Would they consider moving to Hong Kong to run the ICC administrative head office? The previous administrator had left unexpectedly and the administration was severely stretched. It would only be for six months. ICC's office had been established a couple of years earlier near Tai Po in a three-storey village house that provided both office space and accommodation.

They arrived in Hong Kong and were inspecting the new office when the phone suddenly rang. Shane gingerly picked it up to find Harry Hoffmann on the end of the line. Harry needed cash to pay the bills. New to ICC as they were, they had to tell him that money that everyone thought was in the bank… was not there.

Lyndel remembers: "For the previous six months, ICC finances had become a real struggle. The vision was fresh, the children were beginning to flourish in the new Oasis House, David was working very hard making as many appeals as ever, but no money was coming in. We kept praying and asking God why. Why bless this vision with flourishing children, and not release the finances?"

While dealing with the stress of having no funds to send to Harry, they were dealt another blow. Fred, a senior ICC team member, left abruptly. The sudden departure just didn't make sense until everyone pieced together a pattern of strange behaviour and unexplained disappearances that had never quite checked out. There were also clear signs that a moral failure had taken place.

David slowly realized that his friend had much more going on. "I had found out on the very day of the opening of Oasis House that my friend had been lying to me. In being too trusting and naïve in trying to see the best in everyone around me, I had deceived myself..."

The irony was that he had become increasingly proficient at dealing with the games played by government officials. "I had learned to read between the lines of what was said and what was actually being communicated. But I had not expected attacks to come from the inside. The starting point was always to completely trust colleagues who had given up so much to be on the team in China."

David was keenly aware that this might make it harder for those around him to trust his judgment and leadership. More shocking was that "I realized that no one – not even I – was sheltered from the temptation to wander away from a godly life. It was a huge lesson for me not to ignore these signs again."

Once the lies were uncovered, donations to ICC began to flow once more. It was uncanny for Lyndel living through these times. "I had this profound sense that once we had uncovered the problem, shed light on it, and removed it from ICC, then God released the funds. The money was now going to where He wanted it to go."

Shane and Lyndel reset the administration and finances and finally, at the beginning of 1998, they walked across the famous Lowu Bridge with their luggage to take the train to Guangzhou and then Changsha. It was a little daunting passing over the same historical bridge where spies had been exchanged between China and Hong Kong in the 1960s but also an exciting way to start a new adventure.

For all ICC recruits, the ability to speak Mandarin Chinese was key and two years of full-time Chinese language training lay ahead, before embarking on work in the welfare centre. They visited the project just once a week to keep in touch and to provide some specialist advice as necessary. They settled in an apartment near the same university that had blasted Lyndel with propaganda six years earlier. The propaganda loudspeakers were now silent – as if to say that this was a *new* China.

The language teaching was usually done on a one-to-one basis with lecturers from Changsha University but one of the ICC caregivers, Annie, gave her time to be a conversation partner. Chinese methodology was used; that is, no English was spoken at all – just like teaching a baby. Foreigners were expected to learn like Chinese children, with no accounting for a Western learning culture, structure, or organization, or indeed the fact that they were adults. It was twelve months before Lyndel realized that her teacher actually spoke good English.

Learning language the "local" way sometimes caused the students real frustration. Justin Anemaat who arrived a couple of years after Lyndel once climbed onto his classroom desk, rising to his full 6'4" inch height to shout, "I can't do this language!" But he like the others learned to speak it fluently over the next year. You had to – as no one spoke English in the apartment block, or in the street, bus, market, or welfare centre.

The ICC long-term permanent workers were beginning to see a new China that temporary visitors, however often they came to China, could not appreciate. Serving in the field was a real test of strength of character. And in China, it was doubly so.

The missionary experience

For most missionaries, a trip to China was like being forced to look in the mirror. They learned so much more about themselves that it almost transcended their lifesaving work. Harry described it graphically: "You find your own dark corners, and areas of helplessness and fear that you didn't know existed. Nobody believes that before they go. We had to decide the fate of one human being over another."

Feeling homesick just made it harder to adjust to life in China – those who did it best just accepted that it was different. Gertrud admitted, "There were many times when I wanted to return to Switzerland. But the great need of the children in the orphanage, the relationship with the children, the team members, and the local people helped me to endure. I had always known it was right for me to be in this place. It was helpful to remember how I had been called."

Everything was foreign – the language, the culture, the food, the people. Even when you got home it was impossibly hot or freezing cold, and that was indoors. The toilet was a hole in the floor, flushed by a hose, and frequently blocked. Used toilet paper was folded and deposited in a lined bin alongside, as the pipes could barely take the organic, let alone less organic, material. It was easy to forget to tell a newcomer not to put toilet paper down the hole. If the toilet became blocked, the man who cleared the blockage would leave the contents all over the bathroom for the resident to sort out.

The water from the tap (when it was flowing) could not be drunk and was best boiled and filtered before brushing teeth; bottled water was almost non-existent. The volunteers' flats were surrounded by thousands of others and were noisy, overlooked, and smelt of the neighbours' cooking and tobacco. The electricity supply looked dangerous to the eye, shocking to the touch, and could black out at the most inconvenient moment. The entrances to apartment blocks were dark and dingy and heralded a stiff climb; lifts were rare.

You could get little rest. Gertrud noticed: "The noise level of music or television was always on maximum. Loud shouting in the courtyard often woke me up and I could never adjust to loud firecrackers going off suddenly day and night."

She also had to get used to the hospitality. "It cost me quite an effort to try the special food when we were invited to banquets, like chicken feet, frog, turtle, snake, or different kinds of seafood. How do you refuse without offending your host? These are expensive goodies and you can't get away with not helping yourself. Your host will make sure your bowl is full of the best treats."

The family of a staff member kindly invited Gertrud and Angela Walker for a meal, because Angela had given medical help to their grandmother:

> We were told that they would serve us their famous dumplings but of course we didn't just receive dumplings, but a huge Chinese banquet. The host offered us a brownish, homemade wine, which we politely refused but he would have none of it. As I sipped, I naïvely tried to imagine where they were growing grapes. At the end of the meal the host showed us an antique-looking bottle of brownish liquid. To our horror, we discovered a fish and a snake floating in the liquid. Shaken, I congratulated myself on only having taken tiny sips.

Once, Lyndel and Shane's landlord asked them out for dinner, as he wanted to practise his English and show off his new foreign tenants. They looked forward to the occasion, as he offered to take them to a tasty duck restaurant. But when the time came, they were shocked. "We were not served duck. We were served dog, but the landlord's English pronunciation had come out as 'duk', hence the confusion."

There seemed to be no rest in the city as business and building work went on every day of the week. Gradually Sunday became a little quieter but there was, as yet, no weekly routine as in the West. Having to negotiate crowds wherever they went was difficult to get used to, especially if they had come from rural areas back home.

Any movement outside by "the white people" was spied on by hundreds of eyes; they would be mobbed for their light coloured hair and loudly talked about – something they found out when their language skills, and eavesdropping, improved. When Lyndel took her newly adopted Chinese baby Olivia out to the park on a Sunday, strollers would gossip. "You know the reason why Western women want to adopt Chinese babies? They like to keep their figure. By having no babies themselves, they can stay slim!"

It was even better to be able to reply in Chinese. There were invariably roars of embarrassed laughter when it was realized that these foreigners had heard every word. A small crowd once surrounded Justin: "Look how big he is! And his feet! Look how big his nose is!" They scattered in all directions when Justin looked down from his full height and retorted loudly in Hunanese-accented Chinese, "That's the rudest thing I've ever heard!"

The foreigners could not get used to people spitting everywhere and the dirt and rubbish outside around the houses. Yet the Chinese people kept their homes and themselves extremely clean, with piles of shoes left outside the door to keep the floors sparkling.

Many business people thought that all foreigners were rich, so they would try to rip off the volunteers, who sometimes had fewer personal possessions than they. If you understood a little about China's tempestuous history of war and famine over the previous 400 years, their actions were understandable, but it could make the team feel defensive and seem unfriendly, when they were just trying to avoid being cheated.

David came to learn about how Chinese people set their priorities. "There were many 'This is China' moments of enlightened understanding. We had to learn the concept of keeping face and the very different way of thinking and solving problems. To Chinese people, the present moment was more important than the future. When they told you something, this was just about now – you could not conclude any future action from their telling." For instance, they might forget to feed a child. Instead of saying "Sorry, I'll do it now," they might say that they had done so. That would avoid any embarrassment, disappointment, or unpleasantness. They could always catch up later when nobody was looking. That attitude required constant checking and infinite patience. To a Westerner, this was lying but to someone brought up in a Chinese culture, it was a way of not hurting your feelings or being offended.

A few days in the Hong Kong office every now and then was a great refuge where they could spend some time recovering and refilling the tank. They were always made to feel very welcome and it made them realize how much they had grown to appreciate and even love the Chinese people who regularly displayed friendliness and hospitality to them.

ICC continued to move fast, never quite knowing where it would end up but confident of the direction of travel. It reflected David's dynamic and charismatic approach. "Sometimes it felt like being on a knife edge – stressful, as though running down a road that was filled with obstacles, but exciting as the impossible seemed to happen and the children's lives began to be transformed." ICC's strategy was (in the words of Deng Xiao Ping) like "crossing the river by feeling the stones".

A time of challenges

For Harry Hoffmann, leading the work in Changsha, the pressures were intense. Harry had no experience of social work, Tina had been a kindergarten teacher, and they had been in China for just over six months. They had come as hands and feet to help others but they had taken up a task that demanded much more than they could have imagined.

The hushed conversations and worried looks on the faces of ICC's international board members on the night of the Oasis House opening were not shared with the new China Operations Director. Why was he being told that everything was fine? It was nice for David to entrust him with major leadership responsibility almost immediately but he had to look people in the eye if he had to delay paying the bills.

Harry felt that he was not being properly briefed and that made it hard for him to make informed decisions. It undermined his confidence and it made him feel as if he weren't trusted. He began to ask himself why he wasn't being told. Why was it so difficult to get money from Hong Kong, when he knew that appeals were going out to donors? Why around the time of their arrival had ICC become independent from CCSM, and the American couple, Tim and Carmen Tyler, moved back home? Did the singles understand how difficult it was to be a family in the field?

The shock of the sudden departure of the team member would have rocked even an experienced organization but Harry felt oddly relieved knowing the full story. He realized that he would have felt empowered by the truth earlier, rather than just being told that there was no money.

David was a great help when the short-term teams were there but as the leader in China, Harry had to deal with the personal issues of the permanent team, often mediating between the dynamics of families, singles, and denominations. He had to prevent one team member taking a baby out of the orphanage without permission. "God told me that I must adopt this baby in the three weeks before I go back home." Then an older couple scolded Tina for putting a ribbon around one of the children's teddy bears "because it was making the toy an idol".

Their lives had moved from normality to being a struggle and there were few to support or pray for them. They felt very powerful forces overwhelming them. Living in the midst of the work was very wearing. Tina would hear babies crying outside the barred gates of the welfare centre as parents, unable to cope, abandoned them in the dead of night. "As Oasis House moved from eight children to forty-three, we had to decide which kids to take. It was like being Caesar, determining who would live and who would die."

The authorities came to Oasis House to do a mandatory pregnancy test on the women working there. They would pick three at random and if they were found to be pregnant without permission, they would be pressured to have an immediate abortion. "Oh," they said, "and Oasis House would have to pay for the abortion." Harry flatly refused. "Sorry, we cannot do this." They had no power to say no, but could not say yes. Thankfully, nobody was found to be pregnant.

David remembers frequently coming from Hong Kong to Changsha, happy to see the children and to learn of all the new developments. It made life easier that Harry and Tina were doing a great job of leading Oasis House:

> But then I began to appreciate that their responsibility
> was heightened as they had their own children to care
> for too. Sometimes Harry and I would head out in the
> evening and spend hours talking about the challenges.
> I wished I could have done more to support them,

but it was very early days, we were all young and
inexperienced, and I knew that whatever I could offer
them was not enough.

Other challenges arose. The Hoffmanns had to do a visa run back
to Hong Kong every two months with their young family before
ICC received permanent visas for their work. Getting back into
China could be complex. Once it took four months. Another
time their approved and official Hunan Province visa papers were
confiscated by Guangdong's provincial authorities.

Little things could swell into huge disappointments but there
were big things too. They were confronted with death on a daily
basis. Then when they went back to Germany to raise financial
support after a year, they found that nobody had thought to tell
them their church had been disbanded and their funding stopped –
they had been abandoned emotionally, financially, and spiritually.

The biggest stress was brought about by being constantly
watched. Their mail and emails would be opened and read, and
phone calls were monitored. They were limited to certain areas
in the early days and had to let the welfare centre know if they
travelled anywhere – especially to the countryside. The welfare
centre was required to put a staff member, a Communist party
person, to sit next to Harry while he worked. They were meant to
take decisions together. "It is very taxing when every move you
make gets reported back to the government."

Harry and Tina realized that in joining a very young
organization, "We had far too much responsibility at that stage
of life with two little kids." Tina looks back on their enthusiasm
and inexperience: "We were new in overseas missions with no
experience, in one of the hardest places in China. We said yes to
leading the project for a year. But the year never ended because
we were a key part of the whole project at a time when there was
nobody else."

Harry began suffering from chest pains but on his next trip to Hong Kong, Cameron Tallach, the missionary doctor who served ICC patients for free, could find nothing wrong. He put it down to stress, the result of three years' full-on activity.

Tina was looking out of her window one day. "I saw a couple walking into the clinic below, where I knew that they carried out abortions." Some time later they walked out, the man walking in front and apart from the woman down the path. The girl was crying. "It was a picture of the pain of the place, of decisions made so casually over death, and where people were left to suffer alone. The man did not know how to comfort or relate to his wife." Was this a picture of themselves?

By 1998, Harry and Tina were arguing and depressed and sensed that their marriage might not survive. "Did I follow God's will and stay in China – or was it God's will that I leave to protect the family?" Harry even sought advice back in Germany and was convinced that the family came first. It was time to leave. They went to China in obedience with their two, now three, children because they were faithful to their calling. God put them in and God took them out. "We five had to stick together."

More than two decades later, Harry and Tina now run a long-established counselling service in China in Kunming, called "The Bridge". They have helped many ICC volunteers and other expatriate and local people to deal with their personal challenges.

"It took us ten years to make sense of it," Harry says, "to discern how we made our choices, and the pain that came from it – and how to deal with it. It made us realize that we wanted to help those who support the orphans. But to be ready for that calling, we had to go through the valley first."

For a while the questions kept coming. They saw that ICC's desire was to do more than simply save the children; it was to give them an abundant life. Yet it was painful when some were so ill that they had little chance of survival. Was it really worth it?

Or was the pain a part of God's school of personal growth? Why has missionary service led to cases of personal suffering, while at the same time ICC has saved so many lives? Harry wondered whether good could only be done alongside great sacrifice: "Life is not a straight path. It has detours, and the detours can turn out to be the new life path."

Harry sums it up: "The job had to be done, but as young leaders, we needed first to learn from others." He sees himself as a wounded healer – a cracked vessel, broken and repaired. "In that sense the experience was worth it."

CHAPTER 10

Hope House

"I wanted to develop Oasis House into a model that the Chinese authorities could aspire to. Oasis House wasn't an orphanage; it was a home. It wasn't one-dimensional where children just 'lived', but a multi-dimensional place where every aspect – physical, mental, emotional, and spiritual – could be developed," says David. His vision did not stop at Oasis House. Sitting alongside this was a desire for ICC to reach out to those in the Changsha Welfare Centre and beyond.

There were children all over China who needed the kind of love and care that ICC was providing. They had gained a great deal of credibility when the Minister for Social Welfare had opened their new home, and they could build upon this. Welfare centres across China were still places of great suffering for abandoned children with disabilities. Oasis House was the beginning not the end.

For the first time, David was fortunate in having a dedicated pool of specialists: nurses, therapists, teachers, and extra hands and feet to develop new initiatives. Following her language studies, Lyndel felt more confident and her visits to Oasis House became more frequent. She had some reservations but despite the culture shock, language, and the challenges and stresses of being in China, she felt very firmly that this was where she was meant to be.

Therapy, both occupational and physical, was an obvious need, as it could lead to demonstrable improvement to the physical and emotional needs of the children. Angela Walker, helped by a

British short-term volunteer, Sharon Clements, had begun some therapy treatment based on her training as a nurse, but Lyndel was a therapy specialist. She took a blank sheet of paper, and conducted assessments on each child in Oasis House to develop an individualized therapy programme.

Lyndel quickly realized that she needed more than her one pair of hands. She couldn't wait for more therapists to come from overseas then spend the first two years learning Chinese, so she had to train up local therapists.

The work begins

Three young caregivers, who had only been working in ICC for a short time, were selected to become trainee therapy assistants in 1997. They had come straight from the country without even finishing high school. They clearly had no knowledge of anatomy, muscles, and the impact of conditions such as cerebral palsy and spina bifida. But what was important was that these trainees eagerly took to learning. They had a natural ability, sensitivity, and affinity for the children; and the kids loved them.

All three of those very first therapy assistants – Liu Jing Hua, Xu Li Ping, and Peng Ying Hui – are still working with ICC. Lyndel says, "It must have been strange for them working with these foreigners with bad Chinese; and communication was often in sign language in the early days."

At first they just copied everything they were shown even though they did not understand why. "Here's the programme; this is what you do; this is how to do it." It was necessarily basic but it now meant that there was always someone who would be working on therapy. It also demonstrated the benefits of on-the-job training that David had hoped for inside the welfare centre.

Liu Jing Hua remembers that she had no understanding of therapy for children before she came to work with ICC. The first training session was how to feed a child with cerebral palsy. She learned step-by-step, by doing, helped by a natural passion for the children. In the beginning, her limited background was reflected in a lack of confidence but she grew into the role so well that now she manages the therapy department in Changsha, overseeing a team of therapists and assistants. Indeed, one of the assistants, Sun Ping, is a former ICC child.

Liu Jing Hua lives ICC's values on a daily basis, patiently working with children, even if weeks pass without any visible improvement. It's those special times, when a child learns to take their first steps after two years, or starts school, or learns to hold a pen, that make the difference. "We don't just help the children; we learn so much from them," she says.

Foreign staff come and go but ICC could not maintain the work indefinitely without committed local staff like these three original trainees. They will be in Changsha with the children on a daily basis for five, ten, twenty years, or more.

At that time there was no therapy equipment in China and it was very difficult to import. The only equipment ICC had was wooden chairs but children with cerebral palsy couldn't sit in chairs so they had to lie in cots all day. However, in the local workshops they found carpenters, tailors, and machinists who would help to make the tools they needed from pictures in books and magazines. They asked visitors to pack samples of equipment in their suitcases and had them copied in the back-street machine shops of Changsha.

They built up a range of shaped chair seats, like corner chairs, specifically made to measure for each child with cerebral palsy. Children were now able to sit upright during the day and look around. They were angled to provide the proper support, with fitted tables so the children could stretch out their arms and play with toys. They installed padded seating around Oasis House, and designed frames for children to practise standing and walking, all made by local carpenters. They sourced cushioned therapy mats and rolls from tailors, or made their own – and still have a small tailor's corner to do so today.

David remembers the shock of the welfare centre staff when they gave their first mechanized wheelchair to a disabled child. The cost of the chair donated by a supporter specifically for that child was US$3,000. "It seemed a huge amount of money to everyone at the time but, not only did it significantly improve the child's quality of life, it also conveyed to the government and the staff in the welfare centre the value of children, regardless of their disability."

As one-on-one therapy routines were established, ICC developed conductive education classes, assisted by the Hong Kong Society of Rehabilitation. These classes aimed to teach movement and independence in children with cerebral palsy. Small groups of children practised fine motor skills by learning how to do everyday tasks like feeding themselves with a spoon, opening and closing the lid of a tube of toothpaste, or learning how to identify their own possessions in their own drawers and cupboards – a concept still new to most of the children. They all came to love "circle time" as they began to explore their own personalities and those of others.

As the children at Oasis House began to adapt to their new life, the therapy and education provided at Oasis House was beginning to produce dramatic improvements. Although they were quite physically disabled Li Shi, Wang Gui and Wang Hua did not have any intellectual disabilities and flourished in ICC's little school. It was clear that some of the children were ready for mainstream education.

It had been difficult enough getting Chen Shi in a wheelchair admitted to the local government school – which was his legal right. There was an even greater reluctance to admit a child with cerebral palsy who was perceived to be much more disabled. ICC fought hard for Li Shi and was successful, but he had to endure significant discrimination. At first he was even barred from taking exams for fear he might pull down the averages, and he had to struggle to move around school premises unsuitable for disabled access.

Miracles were taking place daily. David remembers "coming in to a therapy session in Oasis House and seeing Zheng Quan rolling around on the floor. I couldn't work out what he was doing until one of the ICC therapists asked me to watch. Then I saw this young boy attempt the impossible. He was tying his shoelaces. The smile on his face when he had completed the task made my day."

A key part of David's proposal to the Civil Affairs Bureau in April 1995 had been the idea that Oasis House brought together residential facilities, therapy, education, and medical care under one roof. Training was a mechanism to transmit ICC's underlying values of love, hope, and opportunity for each individual child in a way that was useful to China.

"Sitting with government officials, I knew that a care home for twenty children just didn't have the scale that the government wanted and would not get approved. And so the idea of making Oasis House a model training facility for welfare centres across China emerged. It was quickly embraced by the Civil Affairs Bureau, along with an offer to promote training across Hunan."

The first training courses took place in the summer and autumn of 1997 and then caught on as other welfare centres became interested, first in Hunan Province, then across China as far as Shanghai, Tianjin, and Xinjiang.

Lyndel's processes were compiled into a *Therapy Manual for Carer Training* to enable students to learn the fundamentals and to understand why things were done in a certain way, and it is still used today. Training topics included early childhood development, paediatric care, explaining the importance of good nutrition, hygiene, stimulation, and the importance of physical touch – all provided in an atmosphere of love and care.

"We started from the beginning, assuming nothing. When something was taught, then it was immediately practised in Oasis House. It was a revelation to the trainees to see how the children were treated, and how care created an environment full of warmth. They saw children responding and began to understand what we were trying to do."

Relations with the Changsha Civil Affairs Department grew stronger as their sense of pride was touched by outside welfare centre directors and staff visiting Changsha for training. Aside from the Hong Kong Centre for Rehabilitation, ICC was the only organization providing this kind of training for welfare centre staff in China.

The impact of Chinese cultural deference to seniority was still evident. ICC would visit therapists in the field to see how the training was used in practice. It was notable that if the director of a welfare centre attended the course, change would be imparted from the top down. If a junior had attended the course, it was more difficult for them to influence their home centres. What did stand out was that senior visitors, whether government leaders, welfare centre directors or staff, all noted how the children under ICC's care were often healthier and happier than the able-bodied children in their own organizations.

From David's earliest visit to Nanning in 1993 with Chan Kit Ying, abandoned healthy baby girls were adopted. From mid-1996, ICC began to advocate for the adoption of special needs children after a couple on an ICC short-term team were so moved that they began the process of adopting a child. In 1998, Lyndel and Shane adopted their daughter Olivia from the Changsha Welfare Centre, and a few years later Gertrud Schweizer adopted Pin Pin, a resident of Oasis House.

For the most dependent children, Oasis House would be their permanent family but for as many as possible it would be a transitional stage – one between a life of neglect and a "forever family". ICC teachers and therapists would prepare children in Oasis House for adoption by teaching them a little English, and helping them to grasp what it would mean to live in a family. To date, some 250 children have been adopted out of ICC projects – almost all internationally.

David's travels also allowed him to develop relationships with donors outside China to support children with severe medical conditions. This allowed Zeng Peng and Gu He to have papers prepared for them to go to temporary foster families on medical visas to the United States. However, the authorities refused them an exit visa and Zeng Peng died in January 2000 from a survivable genetic defect. Happily, Gu He was adopted overseas six months later.

Despite the joy and sense of achievement at the opening of Oasis House, and dramatically changing the lives of forty disabled children, it was heartbreaking to work in close proximity to the government welfare centre where hundreds more children still remained in the old conditions. They could not bear to see children so close by pass away from neglect, malnourishment, or preventable illness without even a pair of loving arms holding them as they died.

Gertrud

Gertrud Schweizer in particular had a real heart for babies and toddlers with disabilities in the welfare centre. One Saturday, she took personal care of a boy with cerebral palsy who had acute diarrhoea, but after the weekend she came under pressure from the state orphanage doctor to release him. The doctor promised to give him the same care so Gertrud agreed – but the boy died within days.

Gertrud took it badly. "I felt that I had put the relationship with the doctor before the needs of the little boy." She was even more shocked by the doctor's comment: "If the boy had recovered from this illness, he would still have not been normal."

The system had made the doctor callous enough to say that it was better for the boy to die than to live. The doctor explained that she only had a tiny amount of money in her budget (¥10 a child per month, US$1 at the time). She therefore had to use it on children strong enough to be able to recover themselves.[9]

That evening, Gertrud settled in her small apartment in the welfare centre and wrote a proposal to David outlining a potential partnership between the government and ICC to raise the general standards of care so more children could be helped. On receiving the proposal, the welfare centre felt that it was not ready but instead agreed to give ICC several rooms inside the centre – which were in a state of advanced disrepair.

Gertrud wrote about how excited she was. "I loved to plan and oversee the renovations and to furnish the place. I am very thankful to Yang Hai, a local ICC employee, for supporting me in this task. He does a lot of investigating and purchasing for me and accompanies me to buy all the goods needed."

Hope House, built out of the run-down rooms, was "soft-opened" in February 1999 when thirty-nine babies moved into ICC's care. This rapidly grew to eighty-two children, which, including the forty children in Oasis House, took the number up to 121. The children were no longer tied to their potty chairs and were able to play during the day. Babies were stimulated through overhead mobiles, brightly coloured walls, and music. They sat at tables for their meals and only then did many learn to feed themselves. Most importantly, their ICC caregivers took turns to just hold them.

Gertrud was rushed off her feet. "The ladies training with us in Changsha are coming to help after their lessons. Even David Gotts is among us feeding a child… We are happy after nine in the evening when the kids have been fed and put to bed!"

It was a bittersweet time in that many babies made such good progress in Hope House that they were regarded as being healthy and so were taken back into the welfare centre. For some, they could now be adopted out of the centre; for many, it meant that they would simply deteriorate under the lower nutrition and standards of care.

Relations with the welfare centre were generally harmonious but David remembers that "one day fifteen children were suddenly taken from Hope House back into the welfare centre, without telling us. Gertrud was especially upset, as many of the children still needed the intensive assistance provided by Hope House. I had to tread a delicate path between reflecting the impassioned ICC staff and an unemotional negotiation with the welfare centre director so that he would not lose face. Often we could only pray for the children who were taken from us."

Gertrud continued to focus on upgrading standards. "I submitted a proposal to the supervisor for a new shift rota that would better meet the needs of the children. The supervisor agreed and planned a meeting for all staff – and then she completely ignored what we had agreed! We must remember that we are still guests of the welfare centre with little authority for the children – most of the time we have to battle."

Gertrud still keenly felt any losses, for many of the children had long-term ailments. "I saw that Hu Hao [a boy who had been in the welfare centre for many years] was deteriorating and refusing to eat. I was too busy managing Hope House to fight for him – and he died. I was guilty that I had not tried to make the best medical care available for him. I even dream of Hu Hao and it provoked me to do more for other children."

Despite her achievements, in early 2001 Gertrud felt the time was right to hand over the management of Hope House to one of ICC's local leaders, Gu Mei Li. "I am relieved to be released from this huge responsibility," she wrote, "but find it very difficult to let go. It also means that I leave the ICC leadership team, having built up ICC's project in Changsha from the very beginning."

Even though she was still actively involved, she felt lost. "Suddenly I don't know what is happening and I can't give input. Decisions are made and I'm told they can't be reconsidered. I don't do a good job working this through. I feel frustrated – without a role. I don't feel useful any more. I don't matter any more. Inwardly, I've resigned myself to finding a role somewhere else."

Gertrud took a break to go back to Switzerland and after a few months returned refreshed and ready to take a major part in the ICC "Moving On" project that aimed to settle disabled young adults into the community. Gertrud taking a break proved to be a good thing as that particular project came to be of critical importance to ICC's survival two years later.

CHAPTER 11

Living Stones Village

Dawn Gage, who first met David at the Nanning Welfare Centre in 1993, had remained there to develop her own work with children with disabilities. David had kept in touch. "Dawn and I had a strong connection due to the vision that we shared for China's abandoned and disabled children – and she had committed herself much earlier than I."

Dawn and David felt that they might better realize their shared vision for the children if they combined forces and brought Living Stones under the ICC umbrella. ICC was establishing offices in countries overseas to help raise funds and could assist with the administration. Dawn had a strong network among her supporting churches for people and donations.

In addition, both had maturing work in the two different cities of Nanning and Changsha. It would enable Dawn to focus her time and energy on working with the older children, which was her particular passion, while ICC had more experience and the resources to cater for babies and younger children.

Dawn attended ICC's four-month training programme in 1997, the same mission training school that Lyndel had attended. After that, Dawn returned to Nanning armed with a vision to open a centre for teenage orphans with disabilities. Living Stones Village would be a home, a family environment and a school, and would provide opportunities for vocational training and career development.

Dawn asked David to assist with her proposal to the government in Nanning because ICC could offer its experience in Hunan and the organizational backing the proposal would require. They visited Nanning's Civil Affairs Department, the welfare department, and the disability unit to pitch the Living Stones idea but were met with little enthusiasm. Eventually, they were sent to the Guangxi Charities Federation, who accepted their proposal in full. Dawn and David were finally able to establish Living Stones Village. It helped that Dawn's Baptist supporters had already raised money toward the set-up costs and David had secured strong financial pledges from ICC's fledgling national offices.

Yet eight months after their government partners in Nanning had approved their proposal, Dawn and David had still not found a suitable building to move into. Every few weeks David would fly from Changsha down to Nanning. "After beginning our daily search with prayer, we would walk around plots of empty land, crumbling village houses, and buildings that might just have potential. I am a natural optimist, but even I began to feel that we would never find the right place. We even considered an abandoned pickle factory – but the smell was impossible to eradicate!"

Finally, they were shown a disused building that had previously been a centre for coal research. It was a three-storey building a little away from the centre of the city and on two sides it sheltered a shady garden. On one side of the courtyard was a low building for a canteen and sports hall. It was perfect.

David signed the rental agreement on behalf of Dawn after the usual lengthy wrangling with the landlord. "It finally felt good to have a place, and we began to see how this property could become the embodiment of the vision that God had given first to Dawn and then ICC."

The village project is set in motion

Dawn's dream was for the project to be laid out like a village, where older children would live independently in small groups with house parents. The children would be grouped into small units where they could learn to be a part of a family, be valued, and grow in confidence.

Mobile Mission Maintenance, in the form of Graham Young and another large team of plumbers, painters, and carpenters, returned to China, this time to renovate a property to suit teenagers with disabilities. The project was so inspiring that two ICC volunteers from the Netherlands decided that they, along with their families, would take time off and come all the way to Nanning to help complete the remaining practical work that needed to be done over the course of a year.

One morning, before Living Stones opened, Dawn had stopped at the welfare centre to discover a little boy, Wei Ming, with blue lips and fingers. She asked to take him to hospital, where he was diagnosed with a serious heart condition. It was operable but urgent – and expensive. Dawn was faced with a familiar field decision: should she dip into the US$35,000 that had been raised for Living Stones to pay for the surgery, or keep it all for the project? Under normal circumstances, and where possible, the donor must always be approached first before using the money for alternative projects. But in this instance there was no time and fortunately she knew the donor well enough to know that they would have agreed to pay for the surgery.

She made the decision to use a small part of the set-up funds for Wei Ming's surgery. The surgery was successful and they brought him straight from the hospital so that he wouldn't have to return to the welfare centre, becoming Living Stones' first child. This is a typical life-and-death decision that staff regularly have to make in the field. Wei Ming is today a university graduate and has a long-term girlfriend. His entire future changed because the resources became available to him at the right time. Dawn's natural mothering instinct was demonstrated in that one incident, such that all the children from then on called her "Mother".

Living Stones Village was officially opened in the summer of 1999, and fifteen children and young adults aged ten to twenty years old left the Nanning Welfare Centre to be welcomed into their new home. Of the intake 70 per cent had disabilities and 30 per cent were able-bodied – an intentional mix so the kids could help support one another and become a big family.[10] A hard-fought basketball match could have half the team in wheelchairs and the other half being run off their feet.

Some found it hard to adapt to a new way of life and community. Quan Quan was a beautiful sixteen-year-old girl who had been alone for so long that she had already developed strong survival skills. Within two days she ran away, never to return. Most of the kids had spent all day every day in the welfare centre watching television. They hadn't been taught to play, to listen to adults, or to think for themselves. With routine and consistency, the children began to love their new home, and Dawn loved her role as a mother. The children began to go to school and were taught technical skills, including sewing and how to use computers.

This was a personal turning point for Dawn, who although she had lived in China for seven years, still didn't have an affinity for the Chinese people. She had stayed for "her kids" because she couldn't walk away having told the children she loved them. It was during the process of setting up the village that she really fell in love with China. She remembers these years being the most difficult and yet the most beautiful time of her life.

It was barely six years since David had visited the welfare centre in Nanning and held baby Rose only for her to die the next day. In that time, ICC had been established and hundreds of volunteers had joined teams, holding dying babies or restoring broken buildings. Now ICC had partnerships with the government in two cities, and provided full-time care for children in three projects: Oasis House, Hope House, and Living Stones Village.

A medical and therapy department had been established, and a committed team of long-term volunteers were living full-time in Changsha and Nanning. Welfare centre staff from across the country were taking part in ICC's training programs. The traditional short-term teams that came in for two to three weeks continued to build on the long-term work and more and more people were being mobilized to go to China to serve children. More than 100 children were flourishing under ICC's care and were blossoming as they received love and learned their value.

David was encouraged, but at the same time he was exhausted. He was based in Changsha, but he was travelling all over the world, raising awareness, recruiting volunteers, and securing funds. With all of the projects running as smoothly as he had dared hope and with a strong team on the ground in China, he felt that even he needed a break.

CHAPTER 12

Transitions

D avid had packed a lot into his young life, and his experiences in his twenties had been quite unlike those of a regular young adult. However, as 1999 dawned, he was facing being thirty with a growing sense of disquiet. "I had been in Greater China for nine years without a break except for the trips I took to share about the work of ICC. People wanted to hear about what God was doing in China, and I began accepting speaking invitations to churches and interested groups all over the world – initially in the UK, and then further afield as word spread about ICC's work."

As he travelled and spoke, he met people in a number of countries who donated money, volunteered, generated ideas, and supplied contacts. They began to form groups dedicated to ICC, which would become the ICC national offices, of which there are now eight that act as support and fundraising centres around the world.

After long periods of travelling and speaking, returning home to China was seldom restful. Living in a culture so different from your own is exhausting – and living in China is especially all-consuming. All interactions take place using a language you never quite feel you've mastered, even though David's rapid-fire Mandarin was better than that of most foreigners. An everyday activity, from opening a bank account, to fixing an electrical problem, to finding drinking water was just plain hard.

He had known little else in his adult life and he realized he had few hobbies, interests, and friends outside of ICC. "Whilst my passion and love for the work of ICC was as strong as ever, there was a yearning for something more. I had hoped to get married but that hadn't happened, and field relationships were not always easy. In truth, I needed some time to process what I had experienced. I sat down with a group of ICC leaders, and shared my desire to take a three-month leave of absence." No one doubted his commitment, and all agreed that it was a good idea. He packed up his flat as the spring of 1999 broke in Changsha.

David knew that he wanted to focus on two things during his time away – deepening his relationship with God, and working through the personal issues that he thought hindered his personal development.

His friends David and Lesley Wiebe in Vancouver, Canada, extended an invitation for him to come and stay with them for the three months. It was a place where the natural beauty of mountains and ocean lay side by side. He was also keen to see if he could study, something he had not done since he left school at sixteen. Nearby Regent College was a prominent theological school where he could participate in courses that would challenge and grow him spiritually, especially as he could do so as an adult student without the pressure of deadlines.

It was a powerful time. "The classes helped me step back and ask critical questions as to why, and what, I believed. It was a chance to learn more about myself by creating a quiet space in my mind to dig deeper and understand what God wanted for my life."

David also decided to have some counselling to try to unpack and understand the events and circumstances from his time in China. "During my counselling sessions, I was challenged to discover afresh who I was. It was the first time I had taken the time to speak with anyone else about my fears; the places that I seldom spoke about, even with those with whom I was close."

David realized that if he only knew himself superficially, then he could only know God superficially. "I was too empty from pouring myself into the work in China. But I couldn't walk away as I loved the work of ICC too much – and what God was doing with it. And I couldn't go forward unless I took a long hard look at the things I had kept inside in order to keep myself going."

He wondered whether he had the courage to look at the parts of his life that he did not want to explore.

It was like the bungee jump that I had almost chickened out of a couple of years earlier. I wanted to avoid the fear that I had of throwing myself off a very high bridge into a ravine. But then I thought that if I ran away now I'd always wonder... My memory would be one of fear, not the freedom of having conquered it. And so I grasped the opportunity and jumped – off the bridge into the ravine! Again I decided to jump, this time into understanding myself.

Through Regent College, counselling, and the friends he made that summer, David came to see that Jesus accepted every part of him, including the dark parts, which He wanted brought into the light, and fixed. "It was the sum of the parts that made me the person that He loved. I felt closer to God than ever before and I recovered my previous passion and energy for the work that I had to do."

David discovered that to be healthy he should have a balanced life with time for interests outside ICC – like original thinking, speaking and writing, things that he hadn't been able to make time for in Asia. And as is so often the case when you stir things up, quite a lot more began to happen soon after.

He had been at Regent College for three weeks when he found himself waiting for a class on "Christ, Culture and Civility in the New World Order" to begin. It was quite full but there was a spare

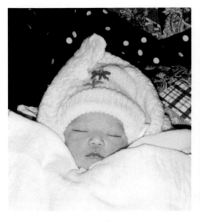

By surviving just a few days, Baby Rose represents the opportunity for life that every abandoned baby deserves (1992)

David Gotts and an abandoned baby during his first trip to Nanning (1992)

Dawn Gage and Chan Kit Ying, Nanning (1992)

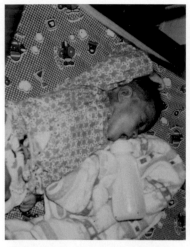

A baby being prop fed (1994)

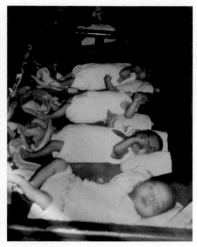

Four to five babies slept in each crib (1994)

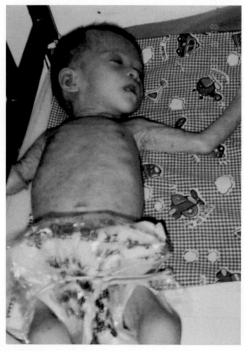

Skin diseases such as scabies were common, as was the use of plastic bags as nappies (1994)

Oasis House in
operation (1997)

David Gotts holding Wang Gui
at Oasis House. Around the table
from the back clockwise are
Li Shi, Liu Guang, Liu Kuang,
Chen Shi, and Su Tie (1997)

Gertud Schweizer with
malnourished child at
Hope House (1998)

Wang Hua, Chen Shi, Wang Gui, and Li Shi at ICC's first school (1999)

Yang Hua and sponsor Helen Harris in Hengyang. This little boy was 'lost' for a year in 2006 and 'found' in 2007 in the girls' room as a pretty little girl (see cover) (2006)

A big smile from a talented, good-looking boy nicknamed "Jackie Chan" (2002)

The Spring Project, Hengyang, first girls' group home: Li Hong, Hannah Chih, Huan, Ling, Mei, Alison Kennedy, Jin, Heng Liang, Ci Ping, Yong Sheng, Xiang Hua (2015)

Wang Hua, the first girl to enter Oasis House in 1997, typing child sponsorship stories on her computer (2012)

Jannene Wall, acting CEO and COO being amused by a child from Sanmenxia (2013)

Ning Kam professional concert violinist accompanied by Sun Wu on the piano at the annual ICC Circle of Hope Dinner in Hong Kong (2017)

Jan Steffan, Sue Munday, Kyla Alexander, Justin Anemaat, Kirsten Britcher, and Lisa Anemaat (2004). This team worked tirelessly in Changsha during ICC's darkest days in 2003

Rich Hubbard with one of the children who attached themselves to him. Rich was the first formal chairman of ICC. He gave his heart and dedicated his life to the disadvantaged around the world (2005)

Lyndel Clancy and Kirsten Britcher with a little boy who was found only to have a physical disability (2006)

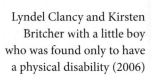

Harry and Tina Hoffmann and family (2008)

Hang Khee Tan holding forth at the opening of the Lighthouse Children's Center in Changsha (2008)

Kyla Alexander, China operations director and founder of the Hengyang Spring Project (2009)

The caregivers are the real heroes of the ICC story, providing care and love to the most vulnerable (2009)

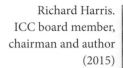
Richard Harris.
ICC board member,
chairman and author
(2015)

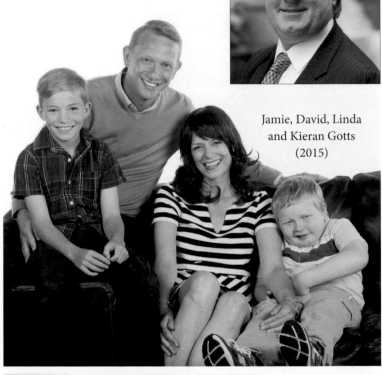
Jamie, David, Linda
and Kieran Gotts
(2015)

The purpose-built
Hengyang Welfare
Centre Project for
disabled children,
designed and run by
ICC (opened in 2015)

seat next to him. The classroom door opened and as he looked up, a young woman walked in. She sat down in the vacant seat. "I was quite pleased that the vacant seat had been next to me. I had been at Regent College for just a short time and knew very few people, so I turned to her and introduced myself. The conversation was brief, as the lecture began."

The professor began by pointing out that the class time was fully his. "No questions please. I do not want to be interrupted while I am speaking."

"OK," thought David, "not a great start."

The professor then proceeded to spend some time criticizing Western missionaries.

"Not wholly undeserved," thought David (a thirty-year-old with a decade of experience working in China) but as the class developed he grew increasingly frustrated at the one-sided perspective.

David remembered that one of the reasons he was there was to be challenged, and to challenge, but too annoyed to stay for further discussion after class he said a quick goodbye to his neighbour and left.

Later that day, he returned for an evening lecture but arrived to find that the auditorium was already full. There were a few seats at the front so, head bowed, he slipped down to the lowest seats and awkwardly sat down. After a few seconds, he looked to his left and there was the same young woman sitting right next to him.

"Hello!" said David excitedly. "What did you think of that class this morning?" His tone already indicated exactly what he thought.

Linda moved uncomfortably close to him. Right in his face in fact. He was used to life in Asia where there is less respect for personal space but this seemed like an invasion of privacy. She loudly whispered, "Sssssh, the professor is right behind you!"

At the close of the lecture, they joked about David's – or perhaps the professor's – narrow escape. David sensed in Linda Tracey something that he knew to be true of himself. Linda had a seriousness about her faith, and yet enjoyed having fun.

As the days spent at Regent College passed, David and Linda became part of a small group of friends that spent time together that summer. And when the time came for David to return to China, they parted but continued to write, email, and occasionally talked on the phone. "We're just good friends," David insisted, when back in China in September 1999.

He respected the grace that Linda naturally exuded and admired her ability to steer conversations to meaningful topics. Embarrassingly, while relaxing at a dinner with some friends, in a moment of weakness he half-jokingly blurted out, "She is a goddess!" – something that he was not allowed to forget. In the autumn, he found himself admitting to a friend, "She is the kind of person I could see myself marrying."

David returned to Vancouver at the end of 1999 for the millennium, to see his Regent friends... and of course Linda.

This time, I recognized a fear in me that caused me to hold back from speaking to her about how I felt. Two days before I returned to China, Linda and I walked along the sea wall in Vancouver's Stanley Park. I remember telling her that there were times when fear held me back, but I could see that fear might also prevent me from embracing the opportunities that God had for me.

Linda's understanding helped me relax and share my feelings with her. At the end of the long walk, we parted. I was no longer walking on the path. I was walking on air.

They were both in their thirties and while David had an obvious call to live in China, Linda had months to go before completing her Master's degree at Regent. The distance would make it tough but they felt their relationship was worth pursuing. David returned to China but they committed to meet in person every three to four months in Vancouver – or wherever else they happened to coincide in the world.

Dilemma

In the spring of 2001 David was on a fundraising and speaking trip to Australia but he was struggling inside. The jetlag was bad enough but he could not sleep due to his dilemma. It was a tough choice: should he stay in China leading the ministry that he was called to and loved? Or should he move to Vancouver to be with the woman he loved? He could either keep the ministry and lose Linda, or keep Linda and leave his heart in China with the ministry he had founded.

He couldn't leave the work he had started in China, but equally he wanted the relationship to continue. He couldn't see a way out, as he clearly felt God hadn't released him to leave China and ICC, but he did not want to end the relationship.

He wrote to Linda from Sydney, sharing his feelings and expressing how he felt. Pressing "send" on that long email was intense, knowing that it might be the end of the relationship. Linda's thoughts were also in turmoil, for while she was open to moving to China, she knew that she did not feel called. She certainly did not want to be the reason that David left China. She too could see no way out and thought, "If I love him, I should let him go."

David has a rare ability not only to give wise counsel but also to seek it. On his way back to Changsha from Australia he stopped in Hong Kong for a few days and went to see Jackie Pullinger, who was an advisor to ICC. Jackie had been working with drug addicts in Hong Kong since being led to the British colony by faith in the mid-1960s. David trusted her to give him sound advice, although he fully expected Jackie to admonish him and say that his Christian work was always more important. He could see her saying, "Follow your call to China and don't stray from it."

As David shared his heart, Jackie's answer surprised him. "David, you see only two options: if you stay with ICC in China you will lose Linda. But if you go to Linda you will lose ICC. I think there may be a third option, but you need to wait for God to reveal it."

He had never thought there might be a third option, and he didn't know what it was, but he was grateful that Jackie had encouraged him to wait with a hopeful heart rather than one in turmoil. Still, he hoped the third option would be revealed sooner rather than later.

Within a few days of that meeting, as the plane took off from Hong Kong back to Changsha, he experienced a direction from God that he had never felt before. He heard a small voice whisper: "Take out your notebook and write down what I'm going to tell you."

The flight to Changsha from Hong Kong takes just an hour, and as the no-smoking light went out and all the other passengers lit up (in the days when smoking on aircraft was permitted), he pulled the seatback table down and began to write. "I wrote page after page. It was all I could do to keep up and get it on the paper."

He had written down ICC's first business plan – a blueprint for the next five years – to develop a structure to steward and expand ICC's resources. It was time for ICC to adopt a formal structure, to further develop the mission's focus, and to formulate a plan for growth and development. He put down his pen as the aircraft pitched down for landing and the table went into the seatback. "I was dumb-struck. God had spoken during the flight because I knew that what was on the paper could not possibly have come from myself."

However, God wasn't quite done yet. The words David heard as the aircraft came in to land were, "And now it's time for you to leave China." He was shocked and tried to take in what he had just heard. "But… where do You want me to go?" I asked.

"Go anywhere you like."

This marked a significant change, for up until then he hadn't felt that he had the freedom to leave. "Jackie Pullinger's counsel had been right. God did have a third option. God had known all along how He was going to work out my relationships with both Linda and ICC."

David could see that he had a team in China who were already providing leadership. Shane and Lyndel, Sue Munday, Gertrud Schweizer, Justin and Lisa Anemaat, Australian graphic designer Kirsten Britcher, and several others were ready to take on the work. They deeply understood and held the ICC values. He remembered his own call back in 1989, a decade ago, when he was on his YWAM course:

1. To go to China.

2. To mobilize people to go to China.

3. To train people to go into China to work there themselves.

David's role was now to concentrate on the second and third phases, as the founder. To do this, he would have to make sure that the nascent national offices around the world were developed enough to grow their resources to send money, materials, and, most of all, people to China. ICC needed to become a robust organization to steward these resources as they came through. David's leaving China was part of God's plan.

In a very similar way to his early decision whether or not to help disabled children in China, he felt the same freedom to choose: "Go wherever you like and I will bless you." He knew God wasn't forcing him down a certain path, but He was giving David the freedom and responsibility to make his own decisions.

His time away had helped him step back and look at the bigger picture, the strategic development of ICC, and how to balance growth and opportunity. If this transition didn't take place, ICC would not grow beyond the existing work in Changsha and Nanning. It had been too difficult to plan for expansion and growth in China because the needs in front of him were always too urgent. There was never time to stop and think. The demands of the projects were endless and one could not say no if there was a malnourished baby who had no one else to feed it through the night. The projects needed to have an organization around them to raise funds, volunteers, and resources if they were to expand into other parts of China.

Blessed as he was with leadership skills, experience, a grassroots knowledge of the work, and fluent Chinese, David knew those talents could also be used in the wider world so that ICC could become an organization with a global reach. If he just focused on the needs of the field in Changsha, rather than on the needs of the whole organization, ICC wouldn't be able to grow.

When David suggested to his team in China that he would move to focus on growing the organization, they felt sad to lose a leader and teammate but he would, in any case, continue to return to China on a quarterly basis to stay familiar with the team, projects, and, critically, to tend the relationship with the Civil Affairs Bureau.

Some may say that he was taking the easy way out – to leave others in China to work on the ground in difficult conditions with sick and dying children. If David found himself, as he often did, second-guessing his decision, he turned back to what God had said on the flight from Hong Kong to Changsha. But that did not stop him living with a nagging guilt for years afterwards – of feeling that he had left his friends behind. "I had held babies in their last hours of life, feeding them when otherwise they would have died. I had been intimately involved in the work throughout my twenties, and had felt the weight of that responsibility and pressure. Much of the pressure wouldn't change; I would still be running ICC as the Executive Director from Vancouver."

David left China in December 2001, and he and Linda were married in Vancouver on 25 May 2002, surrounded by the ICC family and their friends from all over the world. He felt it was God's perfect plan that his marriage was woven into ICC, and that ICC would be woven into his marriage. "That's the goodness of God. He allowed both to co-exist – the third option."

He determined from the beginning to set an example of a balanced life so as to have a healthy relationship with his wife and children – it was tempting, being out of time zone, to work all night. Nevertheless, David returned to China every three months for two weeks – proving that "you can check out of ICC, but you can never leave". The experiences of caring for abandoned and disabled children in China were hardwired into the soul.

ICC was set fair to grow and embrace the future. "I was excited for the future. We had a strong team, everyone was preparing for growth and there was a positive buzz in the air." Yet, within a year, ICC would face three major crises, leaving the organization shattered, demoralized, and feeling betrayed, with a mountain to climb just to keep the work going.

CHAPTER 13

Dispute

Throughout 2002 and into 2003, David worked from Canada, travelling to China every three months to meet with his team. He was working well with the project managers in China, and the office managers around the world, and communicated with them daily. The internet had dramatically reduced the cost of doing so – especially with a newly invented application called Skype.

He recalls, "One area of concern was that serious cracks had appeared in the relationship with the Living Stones project in Nanning. Dawn Gage, Living Stone's founder, had been diagnosed with cancer in 2001 and had immediately returned to America for treatment and recovery."

After eleven months, she returned to Living Stones only to discover that she had been replaced as the executive director by the acting manager, who had been appointed in her absence. ICC's Senior Administration Director, Aaron,[11] who looked after Living Stones, felt that the manager should continue running the administration while Dawn focused on the children. There were also lingering concerns that the stresses of running Living Stones might have an impact on Dawn's recovery.

Dawn refused any diminution of her role. Aaron added fuel to the flames by blocking any further discussion and refusing point-blank to give her back the leadership of the project that she had founded.

"This was very unlike my previous experience with him," Dawn noted. "He had become very controlling after David left and I was not allowed to negotiate with him as an equal." She did not think to talk to David directly and as the interactions went on, she lost confidence in ICC.

When he found out how bad things were, David flew to China in the spring of 2003. He had heard and understood both sides of the story – but how could he choose? Pure administration was not Dawn's strong suit, but he could clearly understand from his own perspective how losing authority over her work at Living Stones would hit so hard.

"Arbitrating this situation was the most challenging task I had to undertake in the ten years of ICC's existence," David said. "It was harder, in that the positions were already entrenched by the time I heard about it and I had not been close to the circumstances that had brought it to a head. I was saddened that it was the first time that I was faced with two leaders who could no longer see each other's perspective."

In Christian circles, the accepted way of handling disputes is to pray with open hearts so that opinions might be changed and unanimity reached. Nothing like this had happened before.

It did not help that by the time David flew to China to help resolve the conflict, the relationship had broken down to the point where Dawn had been told that she could not enter the Living Stones premises. Having already been away from "her kids" and fighting cancer for almost a year, she found this painful and terribly unjust. "I grieved for the time that I was losing with the children, and I grieved that the project was being taken away from me."

In the end, David agreed with the perspective of Aaron, who was of the view that if Living Stones was to thrive, then it needed the skill sets of both Dawn and the local manager. Dawn would be freed up to step into the role of "founder".

Dawn was distraught, and refused to be treated in this way. Her project, the one she had been given a vision for thirteen years before, was no longer under her control. "I was not going to stand by and allow someone I distrusted to take over Living Stones Village." She had grown it into a thriving home for children and she wanted to focus on their needs and the future development of the project.

Dawn could not believe that, despite being old friends, David was unable to see her point of view. After all, it was her work that had prepared the ground for David's own commitment to China.

After a week cooling off in Changsha, David and Kirsten Britcher travelled to Nanning to meet Dawn to see if there was a way to resolve the conflict that threatened ICC, but the cooling off time had merely convinced Dawn that Living Stones Village should break away from ICC.

The difficulty was that David had signed all the joint venture agreements between ICC and the Chinese government, and Living Stones Village was officially an ICC project. David had the legal right to ask Dawn to leave and for ICC to retain full control of the project.

"But could I do that? Should I do that? I spent a sleepless night asking for wisdom. I wanted to hang on to the project because losing this part of ICC's work would be devastating to me. This was the city where I had first held little Rose – the baby that inspired the work of ICC. I also felt God challenging me to open my hands and let it go."

A decision is made

David explained the dilemma to ICC's board of directors. They too agreed that ICC should allow Dawn to take the project in the direction she wished. They would let go and trust God with the work.

They used the analogy of the wisdom of Solomon displayed in 1 Kings 3, where the baby under dispute would not be cut in two to be shared equally – but would be given whole and freely back to the other person.

"The next day, Dawn and I sat down to discuss the decision I had reached. As I shared what I felt God was saying, I could see the relief on her face. I wondered if she could see the pain and sadness on mine."

David and Dawn agreed that over the next three months Dawn would register her own non-profit organization. David would return to Nanning and together they would go to the Guangxi Charities Federation and re-register Living Stones Village under the name of Dawn's new non-profit organization. Dawn would be free to take Living Stones Village and continue the work with the children under the care of the project.

The incident still rankled with Dawn for, despite the agreement, she was still not allowed to step foot in Living Stones Village until the legal agreement had been transferred. It really hurt that in her time of need, she felt badly treated by ICC, including by some ICC board members whom she liked, respected, and trusted and who weren't even living in China. It left her deeply shaken.

Nevertheless she set to her task of establishing a separate NGO in Hong Kong with a board of directors made up of those who had always supported her. With her strong personal links to the local government, she completed all of the paperwork well inside the three-month deadline.

Dawn was a single woman in China with few people to talk to on an independent basis. The friends on her new board had stuck by her and believed in the work of Living Stones. She was then surprised and torn when her friends and new directors began to put her under pressure to submit the paperwork to the Charities Federation herself. This would transfer the whole project to herself in advance and behind the back of ICC.

Eventually she allowed herself to be convinced and without telling David, she went to the Charities Federation and explained what had happened. The government expressed openness to arranging the transfer but she was told that David still had to make the formal request. So a few weeks later, by now the summer of 2003, David walked into the meeting to request that the project be transferred to Dawn's new NGO.

He had carefully rehearsed how to make his formal presentation to the government leaders. It was yet another meeting but they all had to be done properly and, as with every meeting in China, they would be their normal polite and contained selves.

> This was different. I had to sit there while they yelled loudly at me for how, in their opinion, I had treated Dawn so badly – especially as she had just battled cancer. There have been few times when I have seen government leaders so angry. I sat there helpless, knowing that there was nothing I could say or do to argue otherwise. Doing anything more than simply keeping my cool and my head down would further ignite their indignance. I finished up the business of the transfer as quiet as a mouse and returned to Changsha feeling wounded.

Dawn was relieved to have her children back in her care, but in the process felt terrible that she had undermined David – whom she had always trusted and admired.

David grieved the loss of his long friendship and working relationship with Dawn. It would seem irrevocably broken, until several years later when they met up in Vancouver. The passage of time had exposed the pressures that both had faced and gave each time to find out the other side of the story. The reconciliation was a blessed time and they experienced the beauty of how God could heal something that had been broken. Making peace with each other was important to each as events moved on many years later.

It was the first time that ICC had experienced real conflict within its leadership. But there was little time for the wound to heal; more was to come for David. "Before I could really resolve it, we were hit with a much more serious crisis."

CHAPTER 14

Betrayal

The door slammed and the partitions in the office shuddered – along with the staff, who looked down at their desks. Tension hung in the air and a heavy mood hovered over the office. In fact, to Kirsten Britcher, there seemed to have been a cloud hanging over the place the whole time she had been working in the Changsha office. Aaron's behaviour had become increasingly erratic and no one could figure out why.

"I don't have to take this," thought Kirsten, with her Aussie "can-do" spirit. "I've never been treated like this before and I wouldn't put up with it anywhere else. I didn't move to China for it to happen here." The catalyst this time had been the news that the Civil Affairs Bureau had cancelled a meeting – nothing to do with Kirsten, but today she was the lightning rod and had taken the brunt of it.

After six months of witnessing Aaron's outbursts she had a fleeting thought to pack up and move back to Australia, but immediately caught herself. She had come to Changsha from Adelaide two years earlier to serve the children of China and, whatever else was happening, that was the higher goal.

David was aware that the administrative director, Aaron, a long-term ICC volunteer, was having personal struggles at the end of 2002:

> I knew that living, working, and serving in China adds
> unique stresses to any individual and I had seen the

pressures build on Aaron. The thought crossed my mind that perhaps he had had enough of China. Maybe it was time to ask him to leave the field? But it would be really tough, even unfair, after the commitment and dedication that the family had shown to ICC.

David put the thought out of his mind as he knew that it was not uncommon for someone to go through a difficult patch, particularly as they were constantly barraged with people and resource needs, sick children, financial shortfalls, and conflicts in a different culture. He resolved again to do whatever he could to support his staff members if they went through difficult times.

David and Aaron had spoken daily, but the calls became less frequent; there were more and more excuses not to take calls, and Aaron replied to fewer emails. He stopped asking for advice. David felt increasingly shut out. There was always a problem or a roadblock. His friend was constantly frustrated and admitted that he had some difficulty coping. He had become unpredictable at work, and was becoming controlling, distant, and verbal, with a low trigger point.

At one leadership meeting, Aaron had reacted so emotionally to a particular issue that they could not continue. The organization felt weighed down and the work around the administrator gradually became dysfunctional.

David dealt with each of the concerns as they arose, sending resources and support, but nothing seemed to relieve the pressure. The atmosphere began to affect ICC's relationship with their government partners. A new Deputy Director of Civil Affairs, a person critical to ICC's future, had been appointed in Changsha. A sense of offence began to infuse the relationship.

David began to spend more time in China to try to help on the spot. "After one particularly difficult meeting, I happened to see Aaron and a local project manager leave in the same taxi. I silently prayed a short prayer that if there was anything hidden that needed to be exposed, God would bring it out."

The atmosphere was already thick with tension, and David hoped that suspicion and reality were becoming confused. Aaron had been with ICC for some years and had handled a number of difficult situations in a responsible manner. They had worked well together to make the organization more mature and he wanted to trust him. Yet David left Changsha for Canada with a nagging suspicion that something was not right.

Heart for China reignited

Kirsten Britcher had applied to join a short-term team in January 2000, exactly a year after her father had died. His death from cancer had shaken Kirsten deeply and while she was processing it, she had a call out of the blue. "I couldn't hear anything of course, but God's message to me to go to China came in an almost audible voice."

She shared this with a friend whose uncle was a pastor. He told them of a mission in China called ICC, and within a short time the friends had both applied to join one of ICC's volunteer teams. The China that greeted Kirsten and her friend was not pretty. It was grey, dirty, and very cold – to the point that they put hot water bottles down their trousers when they went out.

The short-term team was divided up into pairs and because there was an odd number of people, Kirsten found herself on her own with a room of toddlers. "I'll roll with it," she thought with characteristic aplomb. She bonded quickly with the children and the care staff because she was alone.

There was one little girl she absolutely fell in love with and could happily have adopted. "However, I discovered she was soon to be adopted by a family in the US, which was wonderful – and heart-breaking!"

That little girl placed in Kirsten's heart the passion for ICC's love, hope, and opportunity for such children. Even before she left China, she knew she had to come back and help in some capacity.

Kirsten is elegant and has a very positive character, so she struggled with the stereotypical missionary image of being dull and having no personality. "Wearing flowing, flowery dresses was just not me. I was too much of a rebel. The 'M' word was like an 'F' word to me!" But Kirsten explains:

> God left it to me that it was entirely my choice and whether I went or stayed, both would be OK. But I knew that I would regret it if I did not give it a go. I felt strangely that it would be more risky for me to stay at home [in Adelaide] than to go to China – a country which was so different from the one that I had grown up in, and one of which I had no real idea.

She was worried that because she was a graphic designer, not a nurse, therapist or teacher, that she didn't have any child-related skills. "I found out that it was a God thing. I didn't have typical missionary skills but I discovered that God uses all skill sets, and ICC needed someone with a business mind-set."

So Kirsten left Australia once more for Changsha in early 2001 on the second anniversary of her father's death. There she joined others with a similar calling: Kyla Alexander, Justin and Lisa Anemaat, Sue Munday, Jan Stefan, and Karen Norman.

David remembers them arriving:

> They felt like newbies to me! The first of many long-term staff that would join the work of ICC after I had relocated to Canada. I would only have limited time with this passionate and enthusiastic group but I was impressed that their sense of calling gave them the

motivation to throw themselves right into language
learning and the ICC project. Little did I know we were
raising up the next generation of ICC's leaders.

Kirsten and Kyla became flatmates and set about learning to become Chinese – rehearsing vocabulary, drawing the characters, practising tones, drinking green tea, and eating sunflower seeds on the dining-room table.

After a year the phone rang. It was David. "Kirsten... how are you getting on? And your Chinese language studies? Good... I know that this is a big request, but we need to move ICC's administration from Hong Kong to Richard Hubbard in our UK office. I know you have great business experience... Would you be willing to move down to Hong Kong for six months to manage the transfer?"

Kyla, overhearing the conversation, realized something was up and burst into tears. The happy days of study were over. God was moving on with the work.

Kirsten completed the transfer and moved back to China in the middle of 2002 to work on the Changsha administration with Aaron.

***

An hour after Aaron's outburst in the office and the slamming of the door, he sat Kirsten down to summarize ICC's recent business issues and his proposed solutions. He was polite and unusually empowering – but Kirsten was puzzled. "It sounded more like a handover than a chat!"

She dismissed the thought but within hours, ICC's world turned upside down. David had just arrived back in Canada when he received an email that realized his worst fears. Aaron had just left his young wife and child and moved into his own flat; there was another party involved.

Events then moved at the speed of light. The international team of volunteers met – stunned and shocked – to try to comfort each other. It was clear now why nothing David had tried to do could resolve the director's conflicts. He had been struggling to fix the wrong problem. The stress his friend was under wasn't just related to ICC. David felt sick as events unfolded. "None of us close to Aaron could believe that we had misread the signs. But then none of us could imagine this situation."

Part of the handwringing by those left behind included a nagging guilt of sensing that something had been wrong. "Why didn't we say something?" Why had they not seen what they could have seen? "Why did we not speak up? Why not call him out on stuff?" In a Christian family you don't expect this to happen, and when it does you don't believe it at first.

The team hadn't talked about it because they did not want to believe the worst; they wanted to believe the best of a colleague. That's what Christians do – and ICC was a Christian organization. They had sought to play by the rules; to be loving, gracious and caring; to "give grace" rather than ask the tough questions with a loving heart.

Some acknowledged that they had harboured suspicions but hadn't dared to articulate them. Most felt they might have been able to do something about the situation before it got so advanced. There had been a further worry for some that confronting Aaron with his difficult behaviour might push him over the edge – they were worried for his safety. And yet more than a decade later, Kirsten said, "Not calling him out ultimately did more damage – and didn't help anybody, including Aaron."

Filled with disbelief, horror, shock, and devastation at the news, David flew to China with ICC's new Pastoral Care Director, Edith Watts. Two UK-based pastorally gifted ICC board members, Jean Mclellan and Rich Hubbard, who was ICC's board chairman and the Executive Director of Links International, met them there.[12]

Together they looked to unpick the situation, provide support, and care for those who were hurting so badly. David hoped that after counselling and discussion, perhaps they would be able to resolve the situation.

He had desperately hoped that Aaron would change his mind, but they found him unrepentant. He was firm in his resolve to leave his family and resigned from his role with ICC immediately.

David knew that the China team members would be deeply affected by the break-up of this popular couple that had lived alongside them in the tight-knit community. They had shared so many difficult, happy, and rewarding times together but this was now intense and heartbreaking. David was concerned that it might lead to a pervading sense of distrust – at a time when their closeness had to be so precious.

David needed them to know that he still had confidence in each one as an individual; that they were loved and valued, and that ICC would continue to support them through this time. The pastoral team met each team member to give support as the consequences of the betrayal sank in. What would be the impact on other staff members? And on the tightly knit group of friends who had come to China to build this community? What would local Christians say? What kind of example were they setting to the Chinese?

The biggest question of all was whether the mission itself could survive such a damaging incident. The board of directors was shocked but gave their wholehearted commitment to the work in Changsha. However, a scandal such as this could destroy their credibility with the government – although the cool relationship with the new Director of Civil Affairs indicated that perhaps they already knew.

There is no doubt that working in China was challenging for someone young and untrained to take on a responsibility of such magnitude in a strange country far from home. Harry

Hoffmann had struggled too and he and Tina had asked for help and mentoring. Their decision, correctly, was to leave, going as far as to say that it was to save their marriage.

David remembers Aaron saying several years earlier, when a mutual friend had made some devastating life decisions and walked away from ministry, that he would never find himself in that position. Yet here was the same person making decisions that had at least damaged ICC and at worst could jeopardize its very existence. He had taken no notice of the warning signs or opportunities to turn back.

It took a long time for life to return to normal. Everyone underestimated the impact the crisis would have on them. From time to time they all became aware of thoughts or actions in themselves that were different from how they used to react. David himself did not have time or space to process his own feelings, and pushed them away because he had to be strong in leadership and in ministering to the others.

> I had prayed and prayed for God to intercede, to change
> the heart of this friend who was destroying his marriage
> and family, as well as wounding ICC. Yet it seemed that
> God wouldn't answer my prayer. It didn't seem to hold
> the power that I thought it had. What had happened
> in Nanning, and now in Changsha, left me questioning
> whether God was truly good – or was He simply sitting
> back and leaving us, those trying to serve Him, in pain?
> I couldn't see that God was carrying us. I just felt too
> injured.

A seed of doubt was planted in his heart that perhaps God wasn't really very good after all. He had been devastated by the way that things had worked out with his friend Dawn. Her reluctance to trust Aaron was seen in a new light given the circumstances that had unfolded. Dawn herself regretted not being part of ICC. She realized ironically that if she had worked to ICC's timeframe, and not listened to her own directors, Aaron's departure may have resolved the issues.

However he rationalized events, David's first priority was to pick up the pieces, focus on ICC's core activities, and come out of it as well as they possibly could. He would need even more capacity to face the next bombshell.

CHAPTER 15

Opportunity

I n an immediate reshuffle, David asked Kirsten to step up as China Operations Director. They met with the government partners to introduce the new leadership, which included Sue Munday and a local ICC staff member, Chen Cai Yan, as Changsha Project Manager. China had for a long time given airtime to the equal status of women in professional life but, despite that, the choice of three women to work ICC out of the crisis surprised the welfare centre officials. It proved to be an inspired move as they rose to their responsibilities.

Kirsten herself felt ill-equipped to take on such a task. She had never managed a team, let alone one in a crisis. She had been close to the relationship with the government and was unique in ICC in having business experience. She had good relationships with the China expats and the local staff as a close and trusted friend. On the other hand, she had not been involved with the work on a day-to-day basis. Her Chinese was good enough for meetings but not good enough to review legal contracts. Many of the other volunteers had been in China considerably longer and knew it better. But David was a difficult man to refuse when he recognized that Kirsten had a heart and the ability available to accomplish what he was asking.

She was happy to step up. "I'll give it a go," she said – on the condition that she would be an interim, turnaround manager and that ICC would soon find a permanent director. She would fill the gap, although she felt that her commercial training better fitted her for marketing and communication. But as it happened, "soon" turned out to be in three years; communications would have to wait.

Kirsten led the organization instinctively. She sensed that her role was not about running the operations or directing others; it was about recovery and healing. It was about rebuilding trust in the work, trust within the team, and trust with the welfare centre. For her, it was less about scheduling therapy sessions and organizing the accounting, and more about relationships. She was blessed too as other ICC team members took on responsibility for leadership, including Justin and Lisa Anemaat and Kyla Alexander.

Only full transparency would restore confidence, so Kirsten brought senior Chinese staff back onto the Changsha leadership team. She sought to ensure any decisions were clear and made by people whom all sides trusted. This improved communications and hastened stability, as people didn't feel as left out. Kirsten felt that she had to give individuals the space to step up and to empower them. She wanted to manage and not control, to be strategic but also hands-off, and to give the mission back its diverse personality.

Rebuilding the team would have been impossible without teamwork and partnership. Her new Chinese assistant, Yang Hao, was a true blessing as a colleague and friend, as was Chen Cai Yan, the newly appointed project manager. Cai Yan attended meetings at Kirsten's right hand. After a meeting with the government Kirsten might say, "I think that went rather well," only to be met with a shake of the head. Sometimes Kirsten would leave a meeting disappointed to find that Cai Yan was delighted.

David and Kirsten spoke daily together to develop a vision for the future. His experience made him the ideal sounding board for day-to-day field issues. Leadership could be lonely, especially as she was now privy to confidential information. She now had to make leadership decisions affecting friends who until recently were her peers. But no sooner had the future plans been settled when things began to change in a way that no one could have foreseen.

Transformed lives

Oasis House and Hope House had witnessed the incredible transformation of a group of 121 children as they moved from death to life, from malnourishment and neglect to being healthy, loving children who were receiving an education, medical care, and therapy.

By 2003, the project had seen six years of miracles: children smiling for the first time, children learning to stand and walk, children with disabilities going to mainstream schools with able-bodied children. Some children had been adopted internationally and were now part of a "forever family". One or two older teenagers had expressed interest in being trained as therapy or teaching assistants. Oasis House was a training school for welfare centre staff from across the country, and Hope House for babies and toddlers was flourishing.

Throughout the various ups and downs, the children had continued to receive life-changing, high-quality care. ICC had a settled team of dedicated local staff who believed in the vision and executed the mission. Some of the welfare centre staff and directors were themselves visibly moved by ICC's example of determinedly child-focused, grace-filled care.

Changsha may have been the industrial capital of Hunan Province but in many ways it was still a rural city, surrounded by the lush farmland of the Xiangjiang River as it flowed north to join the Yangtze. As the nearest big city to Chairman Mao Zedong's birthplace, its politics was still very red but in the eight years since ICC had set up in the welfare centre, shanty towns had been replaced by tower blocks, cars had replaced bicycles, and dirty smoky buses were to be seen everywhere.

Oasis House had been given to ICC in 1995 as a derelict shell but had become a tiny oasis in the heart of the city, increasingly surrounded by rapidly rising concrete skyscrapers. The little one-storey building, home to disabled children and surrounded by a garden next to the Changsha Welfare Centre, now sat on land that had multiplied in value many times in just a few years.

David and Kirsten were called at short notice to meet with the new director of the Changsha Welfare Centre in January 2004. They knew that after the recent events it would be a difficult meeting. Their friend Director Zhou had moved on to another role, and they missed the friendly relationship they had built with him, as well as his heart for the children, which had been maturing since his early days with ICC.

With the fast pace of growth all over the city it was inevitable that at some point Oasis House would have to move. The team even had a draft plan that Gertrud Schweizer and Sue Munday had drawn up to move the children into group homes, called "Moving On".

This was a new concept whereby small groups of children of a similar age and the same sex and disability would be brought up in a family atmosphere, in apartments within the local community. This was a big project and it needed some thought and organization, so the team had been preparing the plans for about a year. However, as there was no immediate change in the air, they had no firm timing in place.

David and Kirsten guessed that the meeting might be about Oasis House and whispered to each other as they waited in the smoky boardroom for the meeting – but their thoughts were well off the mark. "The director of the welfare centre came in accompanied by the Deputy Director of Civil Affairs, which made me a little uneasy, as the senior man had lost face in a disagreement with Aaron in an earlier meeting. I tried to open with a warm greeting – but was cut short."

The deputy director abruptly said, "Thank you for your help with the children but we need the space for a new building – so you have to move, immediately."

"How long have we got?" gasped David.

"We want you out by next month. You can take the children somewhere else but if you cannot do it in time then we will withdraw them from ICC's care and take them back to the welfare centre."

Shell shock

David and Kirsten were shocked by the way they were given the news and, in a daze, they walked the short distance from the welfare centre to Oasis House looking bleakly at all the hard work that had gone into the house, the playground, the gardens, the paths and fences. At the very least, over forty children were about to lose their home.

It was clear now that Aaron's actions had affected the relationship with their government partners. Now, rather than having an ally at the Civil Affairs Bureau, they were dealing with an offended official who had no problem treating them with bureaucratic harshness. They were foreigners. He didn't need them, but he needed the site. The Deputy Director of Civil Affairs had no compassion for the children or interest in how they would find a new home. His instructions were to clear the site and to move the children on quickly so that the contractors could start bulldozing in order to build an income-producing home for the elderly.

David went back and asked for more time. The response was a straightforward no. This was the ultimatum, and if they did not adhere to it, then ICC's precious children would be taken from them to return to a welfare centre that had not changed much in the eight years they had known it. Woefully understaffed, they knew that not only would ICC's children with disabilities not receive the care they needed, but for the fragile, it would mean certain death.

Still reeling, David and Kirsten were invited that night to dinner with the management of the welfare centre. "This is China," thought Kirsten. It was a supreme irony – now that the business had been dispensed with they wished to eat a meal together with them. They ate mechanically, while the government officials acted as if nothing was out of the ordinary.

David sat in angry silence. "After six years of demonstrating how the children we cared for could grow and develop, it seemed that it meant nothing to those who were supposedly our 'partners'. I was furious at how the children were being used. As the officials from the welfare centre laughed and joked over dinner, it was all I could do to stop my hands from shaking."

He had to get through the meal and control himself, gather his composure, and begin to think through the next steps. "I knew China well enough to know that all future negotiations would depend upon the goodwill generated by being respectful, despite how I felt. If I was openly angry the officials would lose face and that would undo all the work of the last nine years."

After dinner, they returned to the team and told them the news. "I was so frustrated that we were under so much time pressure to place all the children into new homes," says Gertrud. "I felt that the children were neither valued nor respected – nor our work."

Disappointment turns to opportunity

It was a long night as they talked and prayed, dreamed, and brainstormed. No one believed that it was time for ICC to leave

Changsha. The Chinese character for "crisis" 危机 is made up of two characters meaning both "danger" 危 and "opportunity". 机 They saw this latest situation as an opportunity to develop something new and innovative. Whereas the other two crises had hit them in such a way that response was futile, this situation was one where – by acting fast – they might turn danger into opportunity.

The character of the group homes began to take shape. They decided that it was the right time to execute the "Moving On" plan. They would integrate the children into the local community by dividing them into the smaller groups to receive family-style care.

Out of the ultimatum to leave came excitement. It was a stressful excitement, but they felt positive. The family care concept would reinforce the idea of helping each other out and developing ties that would last. There would still be plenty of interaction between the "families" too, to encourage the notion of being one big extended family.

Moving into the community would not only help the children learn about the outside world; it would help members of the community interact with those with disabilities. Keeping children excluded inside a welfare centre reinforced the idea that people with disabilities couldn't live normal lives as members of society. ICC wanted to lead the way in moving welfare centres away from the concept of large institutional orphanages. Small groups of children integrated into the community would allow them to begin the journey toward inclusion, reducing the "us and them" mentality that seemed to exist outside the walls. A number of the children were now teenagers and there was a need to teach them independent living skills. Integration into the community might also make it easier to take the next, and indeed ultimate, step toward ICC's work being handed over to fully trained local people.

In 2003, this was a pioneering and innovative plan. Only

after the very successful 2008 Paralympics Games, which took place in Beijing, were people with disabilities more commonly seen in public.

David tried to explain the idea of moving the children into group homes to the director of the welfare centre, who could not envisage why ICC wanted to develop into this model of care. It was more expensive to look after groups of children in multiple locations. The director demonstrated that it could be done much more cheaply by holding up a cup. "If I have to manufacture one cup, it is expensive. I might as well make 100 cups. It's much cheaper. It's the same with children. Wouldn't it be better to put 100 children in a home than ten children?"

The concept of family care being key for the healthy development of balanced individuals was lost on him. Still, the director agreed, it would be ICC's resources that they would be wasting and he said that if it was completed within the timeframe he had given them to leave Oasis House then he had no objections.

Kirsten, Sue, Gertrud, and the local team were tasked to find space first for forty children; the Hope House children could stay in their rooms inside the welfare centre for now. They scoured the city and viewed hundreds of apartments but none seemed suitable for children with special needs. It was a slow process and they were frantic. What would normally have needed months to prepare now had to happen at warp speed.

Neighbours, hearing that ICC was looking at apartments in their complex, would severely object to having an influx of disabled children nearby, even to the extent of forcing landlords to rip up signed contracts. Gertrud complained, "How can people learn to understand that those with disabilities have so much to give and contribute?" There was still a feeling that the presence of disability would bring bad luck, or at least might damage property values.

The right apartments had to be on the ground floor or in lift-equipped apartment blocks that were suitable for disabled children. Complexes had to be easy to enter, with wide hallways and doors for wheelchairs. They needed to have at least four bedrooms: three to fit up to eight children, and a room for one or two full-time caregivers to sleep in. These rooms were often more comfortable than the caregivers' own homes.

Sue Munday was a highly experienced occupational therapist, trained in the UK's National Health Service, who had come out to work for ICC, supported only by her savings. She knew all about "This is China" experiences since she had been regularly coming on teams since 1994, finally moving to Changsha full time in 2000. She had already calculated that they would trial the "Moving On" project by selecting one group of girls and one group of boys to move out of Oasis House into flats. They had told the children and teenagers they would be moving, and they excitedly prepared for this new step of independence.

Fortunately, the new welfare centre development was delayed by three months to mid-2004, and the relationship had thawed enough for the director to extend his deadline by that time – giving the group homes project the time it needed to succeed.

Eventually they managed to find two suitable apartments in a district called Sen Yu Jia Yuan and two in Wan Shi Jia. That soon rose to six with two flats found in Hong Xuan. Gertrud was "very grateful for the people of Sen Yu Jia Yuan, Wan Shi Jia, and Hong Xuan that welcomed our children and young people to live in their compound".

ICC was now faced with a new challenge – how would they pay for the properties? If they were going to work within the government's timeframe, they needed to raise US$200,000 super fast. David set to work mobilizing his fundraising network around the world, which by now included the national offices that were beginning to develop. David Sutherland, a board member and a banker/lawyer, chased and cajoled his contacts.

Sue Munday remembers the pressure of knowing that the lack

of money would prevent them moving forwards, despite all their hard work. She will never forget God's miraculous provision as thousands of dollars flowed in during the first few weeks. It was enough to buy four of the small flats and rent two others. They could go ahead in confidence and start moving the children.

The children were involved in the decision-making process. She recalls, "It was fun to take the young people to the market and choose the material for their bedding and curtains. I appreciated the ladies who sewed the items as they respected our young people and were very kind to them."

By January 2005, most of the Hope House children had moved. Gertrud wrote in her diary, "I realized how much support you get in a team and how well we complemented each other. Before, I always wanted to do projects on my own. I experienced a great relief after all the children and young people were installed in their new homes."

After a fast renovation process to upgrade the apartments for disabled children, the first two groups from Oasis House moved into the community. A third and fourth group of eight to ten children per flat soon followed. As the welfare centre piled on the pressure to vacate Oasis House, the team worked frantically to relocate the last groups of children. Their move was very rapid and the team didn't have the time or resources to walk these kids slowly through the transition process. As a result, the first groups settled into their new home much more quickly than those who came later.

By May 2005, all of the children had moved out of Oasis House. Their beautiful home, which had for so long represented an oasis, a light in the middle of the city, took ten minutes to be crushed by a bulldozer. It tore through the playground, which had heard so many happy sounds, and the lovingly manicured flowerbeds. Oasis House was replaced with a lifeless twenty-storey concrete shell that gave no clue as to what had been there before.

For children who have been abandoned, any transition, even

a positive one, can bring back old hurts and traumas. The staff worked with each child to provide the emotional support and love they needed. Children are robust but even today the older kids will say how much they miss their old Oasis House home.

Yet the Oasis was not just in one place any more. The first Oasis had dried but springs of fresh water had multiplied and spread across the city of Changsha. Though smaller, there were many more of them. More people than ever before were now in close proximity to ICC's vision of how to live alongside the abandoned and those with disabilities. The children living in the community were showing their neighbours who they were and what they could do, and they changed perceptions and mindsets as they played in the local playgrounds with local children.

Neighbours saw the love that the children showed to their carers and to one another, as those who could walk pushed the wheelchairs of others. Changing long-standing public prejudices about children with disabilities was one of ICC's main aims. It was a long, slow and gradual process, but this was the start.

Life has many new learning experiences and for most of the children it was a positive step toward independence in running their home and in giving them a sense of family. They went with their caregivers to the market to buy vegetables, came home to prepare them, set the table, washed the dishes, and cleaned the home. Sue remembers being dragged in through the door by two of the kids so they could show her that they had learned to operate the washing machine.

Zhou Li, who was one of the first children to move into the group homes, was originally abandoned just because he was born with a cleft palate – even though it was easily operable, paid for by the state. He spent his early years in a welfare centre with inadequate nutrition and no education, and this had exacerbated his minor disability. He began to thrive in his new group home and begged his caregivers to let him help prepare the food every night. His passion for cooking grew and as he got older he trained in the food industry and is now independent, working as a chef in Changsha.

David's natural optimism allowed him to be positive about the future. "Living through those months was like the best of times and the worst of times – as Charles Dickens described it. The pressure was immense yet the excitement of trying the impossible caused everyone in ICC to step up and trust God in a new way. When we were able to draw breath, we could see that He had demonstrated His faithfulness and provision for the children that were not just 'clients' but family to us."

ICC had taken big hits in 2003, but they were still standing, and they had a chance to rebuild and expand their mission of love, hope, and opportunity for China's abandoned and disabled children.

"In early 2004 I had had a picture taken for my new passport. When I replaced the passport in 2014, I looked ten years older in the earlier photograph – such was the intense stress of facing so many challenges in such a short space of time."

CHAPTER 16

A New Oasis

China had changed beyond all recognition in the twelve years that David had been working in the country. ICC had gone from the "Dying Rooms" to the group homes in a journey that, in looking back, he could not have travelled if it were not for the grace of God.

The eviction from Oasis House and the combined crises of 2003 had not destroyed ICC, as had been feared, but had fired it like clay in a kiln, making it stronger. The establishment of the group homes across the city of Changsha proved that ICC could do the seemingly impossible even with just a small team of staff on the ground.

ICC's board of directors was a group of mature, Christian individuals with a real diversity of background. The chairman was head of Links International – global development specialist Rich Hubbard – while other board members with business experience were David Sutherland, an international lawyer who went on to develop a major charity in the Philippines, and Richard Harris, a global banker. Lyndel had returned to Australia after her time in the field and represented the views of those who served on the ground in China, along with her father Graham Young who still worked for MMM based in Melbourne, Australia. Long-serving board member, business life coach, and pastor Terry Phillips was based in Singapore.

When they all met at their next half-year meeting in the spring of 2004, David took the floor:

We are conscious that we are still healing the wounds
of the past year, but we can clearly see how much God
is transforming the lives of children under our care. We
can see many reasons why we ought to stay put! But the
team in China has been praying about it and we think
that it might be time to start a new project.

We would do this by sending teams into other welfare
centres around China to slowly build relationships with
the intention of establishing a residential team in a new
location. We know that if we are being called to step out
and trust God's leading, then He will provide.

The first step was to write a proposal to the Hunan Provincial
Civil Affairs Bureau for them to recommend three welfare centres
in which ICC could conduct a needs assessment. The three
centres would need to have a large population of children with
disabilities, to have no other partnerships with overseas NGOs,
and they had to be open to short-term volunteer teams. If the
situation seemed to work, ICC would like to follow up with a
long-term partnership that would be collaboration, based on
working together, rather than simply expecting ICC to bankroll
the welfare centre.

David had already seen two leaders struggle and leave ICC
because of the burden of project leadership. But then he had a
chat with Kyla Alexander who "shared with me that she felt
God was leading her to try to start a new project for ICC – even
though she was at first reluctant to tell me". He knew that Kyla
lacked the experience to pioneer a new project, but then again, he
himself had left school at sixteen so he wasn't exactly qualified to
be running an international NGO either:

I could see that Kyla was professional and highly
competent. She had been with us for three years so

she had the language skills and had also been close to our recent challenges. She was mentally strong enough to understand herself and recognize that when the pressure and stress came, as it always did in China, she would be able to deal with it. I saw the spirit of Caleb in her. She was not only willing to go out and do, but she was wholeheartedly committed to placing her life into God's hands.

It was a steep learning curve for Kyla, who had never done anything like write a proposal to the provincial government before. "David was very gracious about my badly written proposal and edited the whole thing without saying a word!"

Kyla had briefly thought about becoming a missionary to China in her early years. As a teenager she felt keenly about the needs of the disadvantaged so she completed a nursing degree. For the next eight years, she focused on her career. "Just because I was a Christian and a nurse didn't mean that I wanted to become a missionary!"

However, in April 1999, Kyla was mentoring a young nurse, Lisa Anemaat, at the Paediatric Hospital Emergency Department in Brisbane. Lisa had recently returned from a short-term trip to Changsha with a group called International China Concern. She was very enthusiastic. Then Kyla's hairdresser mentioned that she too had been on a short-term team to Changsha with ICC. But she still wasn't ready to go to China. A couple of weeks later, she found herself on a church retreat and a lady Kyla barely knew said that she had a thought for her in four parts… "Missions work. Disadvantaged children. Hard times, but a happy Kyla."

The messages became increasingly insistent, so Kyla enquired about the next ICC short-term volunteer team. Gertrud Schweizer led her team in November 1999 and as ever they were amazed at David's youth, energy, and friendliness. It was to be a special trip, not only for the participants, but also for ICC. Members of that team were destined to serve ICC over the next two decades, including Justin and Lisa Anemaat, and Jannene Wall from Australia. Justin and Lisa's children were born and brought up over fourteen years in Changsha, Lucy served over a decade with ICC, and Jannene served as ICC's first Chief Operations Officer and later took on the Chief Executive role in David's temporary absence.

The team gathered in Hong Kong, took the ferry to Shenzhen and the bumpy slow train to Changsha. Kyla loved China from day one – except for the white-knuckled driving on the roads. Changsha's weather was also a stark contrast from that of Brisbane, where you are never too far from the sun. Yet the excitement drowned out any culture shock.

Kyla entered a China that was considerably more developed than when David had arrived eight years previously. There was a growing openness to foreigners, people dressed in modern fashions, and strangers from another land were no longer the subject of stares. Changsha's frenetic growth from a small provincial town to a major industrial city was well developed. They had apartments to stay in, rather than something hewn out of a former office with boxes as furniture. Air-conditioning and heating had come to Changsha, even if the windows didn't fit. The infrastructure, however, was still haphazard, for only the main roads were sealed; the rest were dirt and became muddy rivers when it rained – which was most of the time.

David showed the team around the welfare centre and Oasis House, by now just over two years old. Kyla was impressed with Oasis House. She could instantly see that the children were treated as individuals who were loved. She saw the progress in education and therapy and in loving and caring for children. It was basic compared to what she knew back home but it was still a good working environment. The small groups, the high proportion of caring staff, and the general environment all reflected ICC's values, and it encouraged her that ICC was truly living out its words through action.

On the second day of her short-term team, she found herself pulled toward the welfare centre. "I found the welfare centre a difficult place. I cried a lot of tears because it was just not right." Kyla found it personally distressing – "the physical and emotional condition of the children, their treatment, the blankness of the stares, the way the kids were handled, the dirty clothes, and the poor hygiene", but she saw that God was calling her. "He was stirring my heart in an intense way to see the difference between what was right and wrong."

Ten days into the twenty-day trip she knew she would be back. "It was an emotional time, as I knew that I would have to leave so much behind." She signed up in January 2000 to join ICC for five years. She and Lisa had previously both asked their boss for leave to go to China at the same time, who had agreed, saying, "But don't ever go away at the same time again." This time they were both going for good!

After a two-week orientation given by David, Shane, Lyndel, Crystal Kelleher and Jean Mclellan, Kyla retuned to Brisbane to wind down her old life for a new one as a missionary. "It meant leaving the security of friends, family, career and income for a strange land and relying on the financial support of those who rallied around to allow me to come into the field."

Kyla, Justin, and Lisa began two years of language study and were joined by Kirsten Britcher and Sue Munday. They lived on the other side of the river from the welfare centre and visited Oasis House just once a week, which included a weekly dinner with the rest of the overseas team. On Saturdays they helped ICC team members John and Claire Wadsworth with learning tasks for children and to take them on outings.[13]

Despite her professional nursing skills, Kyla's move from language to projects was unusually gradual as there were already others in place. Jan Steffan was responsible for the medical and nursing side, assisted by Claire Wadsworth. Lyndel was running the therapy team with her local staff. Sue Munday, in her role as an occupational therapist, had started a sheltered workshop in Oasis House. Kyla had no particular role but enjoyed integrating and understanding ICC's various initiatives.

She took over as short-term team coordinator from Gertrud in early 2003. No sooner had she been appointed than SARS broke out in China. Severe Acute Respiratory Syndrome was a respiratory virus that in the early stages was highly contagious and lethal, killing 800 people worldwide and reducing world air travel by 40 per cent. All the volunteer teams were immediately cancelled, which provided some time to think about the future.

David's experience in establishing other projects with the government was invaluable. He had the background and the experience to know what the government wanted to hear. Together, they approached the Hunan Provincial Civil Affairs Bureau, a different department from the Changsha city officials with whom they were still having difficulties. They proposed an expansion of their work and asked if they could recommend three cities for them to investigate. The word got around and the city officials began to treat ICC with a little more kindness. They had started to become nervous that ICC might leave.

Kyla, together with ICC's Changsha project manager Chen Cai Yan, Sue Munday, and Lucy Chua, visited two welfare centres in April 2004 that the Civil Affairs Bureau had identified for them. The first visit was to Zhuzhou, close enough to Changsha to be a suburb, and the second was to Hengyang, a provincial town in Hunan Province, three or more hours' bumpy bus ride south of Changsha.

Kyla, Cai Yan, and Lucy walked into the Hengyang Welfare Centre and immediately knew that this was the place. There was an 85 per cent mortality rate among the newly abandoned sick and disabled children and infants who were brought in.

The conditions in early 2004 were shockingly similar to those in Nanning in 1993. They were just 100 kilometres south of Changsha and yet nothing seemed to have changed in ten years. They were led past two big buildings, one of which housed the elderly and the other healthy baby girls, to a small building at the back of the social welfare centre compound.

The disabled children were housed in a single-storey *siheyuan* (四合院), an old square building comprising several rooms formed around an open, sunken courtyard, where small farm animals would have been kept. Water ran through the building when it rained and drained into the little courtyard, where it would collect and then drain through an overflow. The one squat toilet on the corner of the courtyard was guarded by a damaged green door and was often blocked or swamped by running water. It was a breeding ground for rats and mosquitoes. The whole place reeked of urine. Just outside the building was a rudimentary kitchen open to the elements except for hard plastic roofing that gave shelter from direct rainfall.

In this squalid space lived fifty-five children, few wearing appropriate clothes. Their behaviour was wild and they were either desperate for attention or closed off to the world, unable to interact. At first glance, it seemed that all of the children were boys, but they realized that because they all had short hair and the same clothes, it was hard to tell which were boys and which were girls.

Improvements begin

Three times a day they noticed a tension come over the children. Their behaviour changed. Some would cry, some would disappear. They would become less human, for they could smell food being prepared. When food came out, the children would fight one another to grab a handful of rice and would shove it into their mouths as quickly as they could before it could be taken. If rice fell, they would eat it off the floor, consumed by the thought of something to eat. It was survival of the fittest.

The team tried to manage mealtimes, protecting food from the older kids and attempting to feed the younger ones. Violence abounded as many had lost all ability to communicate in any other way. The children were constantly exposed to death because of the mortality rate of newly admitted, young, abandoned, disabled babies. Several children died each week, and those who survived had no quality of life. These children didn't know what it was like to be heard, or seen, or to have their needs understood and met. The environment had stolen their ability to smile, dance, make simple eye contact, or acknowledge others.

Two caregivers would sit in the courtyard, only interacting with the children if they had to. The outcome was often death; if not physical then an emotional death from inside. "The children were physically alive, but their blank eyes gave away that there was no hope in them."

David recalls:

> Kyla and her team thought that bringing in short-term volunteer teams had worked well elsewhere in ICC and this was once again the best way to get caring visitors to spend time there, to build relationships, and to assess the children's needs (which were for pretty much everything!). It would also allow the director of the welfare centre to get to know us without having to offer a long-term commitment. As always in China, we needed to establish their trust.

Kyla and Alison Kennedy, a physiotherapist from the UK, led the first team of short-term volunteers to Hengyang in August 2004. The team members sat on the dirty floor at the height of a sticky Chinese summer playing with disabled children who always needed a bath, and over the next two weeks learned to stop panicking whenever they saw a rat.

Simple activities like playing games were difficult because the children were wild or unresponsive. Craft activities involving dried beans or pasta were impossible because the children were so hungry that they grabbed at the dried food and put it in their mouths before they could be stopped.

The first short-term teams believed these children were valuable, and deserved more than the lives they lived. They occasionally caught sight of tiny glimpses of hope of what this place could be; they knew their presence was helping but mostly there was not much change in the children. They held little ones in their arms for hours, trying to make eye contact, massaging cream into broken and sore skin, and reminding them that there was someone there who cared for them, loved them, and would protect them. Or hold them when they passed away.

As David had worried ten years before, so now were Kyla and her team concerned that some of the children would die between team visits. ICC hosted eight short-term teams in just fifteen months – from August 2004 to November 2005 – and each time Kyla and Alison became more committed.

Judy Elliott, now ICC UK's National Office Director, was on the second team and spent her three weeks in China in a state of shock. "All the teaching of Jesus was there – in 3D, in full stereo; it was a paradigm shift. It changed my life."

She had a growing family to look after in England but she wanted to do more. "I'd always believed that God wanted to help China and I had supported other China missions in the past." She had not travelled much before. "Here I was in China – stunned all the time. It was loud, smelly, and the air was heavily polluted. People would spit on the ground in front of you, the language sounded harsh, and it was physically demanding."

Judy went with a party to Hengyang Zoo. "It was like a walking freak show – the local people would stare at this large group of disabled children, walking crookedly, swaying uncontrollably or in wheelchairs, supervised by ghost-white Westerners. The animals were in a terrible condition. The main exhibits were turtles swimming in what appeared to be urine. But the kids loved it!"

The children did not know how to interact with loving adults; some would climb all over the volunteers to receive attention, while others hid away unresponsively. "Most of the kids had a pervasive smell of urine and diarrhoea; and an infected smell as if they had some kind of bug. They had thin hair, cold sores, and continual chest infections – and scabs on their hard runny noses that leaked uncontrolled snot. Yet even in the very beginning when it was terrible, there could be a huge spirit of joy inside the children – even in that environment, smiles would go from ear to ear."

There were children who had been so deprived in their very early days that they had just shut down. It made a big impact on the volunteers too. "It was often the members who thought they brought the least to the team who sought out the quietest children and loved them most."

Stomach problems were a major problem because of the lack of hygiene. "These experiences were intense. One child whom we called 'Jackie Chan' had an explosion of diarrhoea… But that child needed to be loved – he was in our hands."

The children were so desperate, so poor and needy, that Judy couldn't help thinking of the words of Jesus, "Whatever you do for the least of these, you do for Me."

During this time, they recalled a number of Bible verses, which gave them a determination to serve the children.

> Arise, Lord! Lift up your hand, O God. Do not forget
> the helpless.
>
> PSALM 10:12

God gave them the assurance to continue with the work:

> For he will deliver the needy who cry out, the afflicted
> who have no one to help. He will rescue them from
> oppression and violence, for precious is their blood in
> his sight.
>
> PSALM 72:12, 14

And He gave them verses to remind them why they were holding dying babies.

> Defend the weak and the fatherless... Rescue the weak
> and the needy.
>
> PSALM 82:3-4

David's answer to prayer for an invitation from the Hengyang Welfare Centre to start a long-term project came sooner than expected. In November 2005 he had the joy of signing a contract to establish a full-time ICC project within four months.

At almost the same time as David was signing his name, several uniformed policemen surrounded a large car outside the Hengyang railway station. Inside, protected from casual view by blacked out windows, they found two women and three babies meeting with top officials from the Hengyang County Social Welfare Institute, the rural counterpart to the city welfare centre. The police had discovered a baby-smuggling ring and were covertly raiding a baby drop. The ripples of this scandal would go far and wide.

The Chinese authorities dealt with the trafficking of babies very firmly. In March 2006, the courts found that traffickers had been acquiring babies from poor families on behalf of some orphanages, encouraged by the large adoption fees paid by the foreign adoption system. Senior members from a wide range of social welfare institutions were jailed or fired.

It was a very good sign that the Chinese government was taking a positive interest in child protection and in regulating the process of adoption. The ICC team had noticed that there had been unusually high admissions of healthy baby girls in the area compared to children with disabilities.[14]

The management at the Civil Affairs Department who had formally signed the contract with ICC were gone by the end of the week. David and Kyla had spent eighteen months building relationships that had suddenly ended and they had to rebuild with new management.

> We were thankful that we had signed the contract before the news of baby trafficking had broken. The scandal caused turmoil in the government ranks, which would normally have led to a withdrawal of talks with a foreign NGO. Instead, we received the support of the new leaders as our reputation could be seen to help safeguard the children and also to assist in raising the quality and profile of care. God's grace kept the door open.

The adoption scandal turned out to be positive for ICC's entry into the Hengyang Welfare Centre. It provided a reason for the government to view ICC as a respectable organization it could partner with – another example for ICC of the power of God and His timing of events working together most elegantly.

CHAPTER 17

Starting a Spring

I n China, there was even a culture shock in moving from the city to the country. Hengyang was quaint and just didn't follow normal rules. Karen Norman often left her ground floor apartment door unlocked, as there was always something that needed to be fixed by a handyman. The local people would casually wander through the house, picking up their (few) possessions while their kids would raid food from the kitchen.

Kyla, Karen, and Alison Kennedy moved from Changsha to begin the long-term work in Hengyang in February 2006 and were soon to be joined by Hannah Chih and Liesel Luscombe. David took an active role in supporting Kyla and visited Hengyang regularly in the early stages of the project. His experience and influence with government officials was invaluable.

Kyla was grateful for the coaching that enabled her to learn how to negotiate with the welfare centre. One of the first requests was for more space for a baby room. "It was provided, but was less than ideal. It was too small. There was no play space, and no proper toilet plumbing. The waste water just flowed out the back of the building and soaked into the wall of the makeshift structure."

The ICC team was given responsibility to care for all fifty-five of the disabled children, from babies to teenagers. They had the faith that this place of death could become a place of life, a home, where children could one day learn to laugh.

Like Oasis House, the Hengyang project came from a promise in Psalm 84:6: "As they pass through the Valley of Baka,[15] they make it a place of springs; the autumn rains also cover it with pools." It was named the "Hengyang Spring Project" from that promise.

It was a real challenge to find local staff that were willing to work with the children, so Kyla and her team worked with the children day in, day out. They were faced with limited resources, awful conditions, and needs everywhere. Kyla wrote that the conditions were overwhelming. "Our first goals on arrival in early 2006 were confined to meeting the most basic needs of human life." They prioritized their tasks to ensure that every child had the necessary nutrition, a safe place to sleep, and received basic medical attention. Only once these most basic needs were addressed could they begin to set up educational and therapy programs.

The most urgent priority was to control the traumatic feeding crisis. Fifty-five wild children grabbed, screamed, and hurt each other when the food arrived; such was their desperation. The younger and weaker children were not able to reach the food and this was one reason for the high mortality rate. The team divided them into small groups of similar age for their meals, giving every child their own food in their own bowl and a spoon so that they could know that it was safe to eat.

On one trip, David stood in the middle of the room and couldn't believe what he was seeing. "The children ate like animals, and when their food was gone, they roamed around the courtyard looking for an old bone to pick up and gnaw on. It was heartbreaking and reminded me of Changsha years before. This time, though, I knew that we could do something about the hunger, chaos, and insecurity."

More caregivers were employed so that the vulnerable children and those with disabilities who could not feed themselves were fed individually. The ICC team introduced a snack system and they began to give the kids fruit, eggs, and sausages several times a day so that meal times were less concentrated. The children needed to feel safe and that the adults would protect them if a stronger child tried to steal their food. Gradually the children began to relax, as they trusted that enough food would always be provided.

The ICC team had also secured an agreement with the welfare centre themselves that they too would provide more nutritious food, but instead they stuck to their budgets and it was clear that nothing was going to change. So after six months, they decided to establish their own kitchen, as they had in Changsha. The ICC kitchen provided meals with more meat, vegetables, and eggs, which were cut into smaller pieces to make them edible for children with disabilities.

One of the old ladies who lived in the home for the elderly, Lin Nainai (Grandma Lin), observed that the babies would thrive better if she could provide soft food for them. Each day she cooked porridge and brought it to the ICC caregivers to give to the babies. The kitchen began to follow her lead in producing soft food.

After a few months mealtimes were less stressful and almost all the children were able to sit down at a table – and even go out into the community – without fighting. The children were noticeably healthier and were putting on weight. One lunchtime, the director of the welfare centre dropped in to see them. He started and stared, and his jaw dropped. "Are these the same children?" he asked.

One example was little Yang Jian Hua, who gained half her body weight in just two months. The nutritional status of younger and newly abandoned children improved, giving them a greatly increased chance of survival. Mealtimes became an important part of the routine when the children were divided into family-style groups several months later.

Kyla noticed: "When we first brought a team to Hengyang, instead of playing, the children would end up sleeping all over the team members." The children were exhausted from having no safe place to sleep at night, and when they were lifted into a cuddle they would immediately fall asleep.

"These children had no family and parents to protect them, and no one to hold them at night when they were frightened," recalled Kyla. "There were only four bedrooms to accommodate all fifty-five children – that was ten to fifteen children to a room." Girls and boys, babies, and teenagers of all levels of intellectual or physical disability were mixed together in each room with little supervision. "It presented a dangerous place for younger and weaker children, who lived in a state of fear."

One Sunday, Kyla was woken up before dawn by a knock on the door to tell her that two of the three babies admitted the previous day had died overnight. The babies had not been thought to be in any danger. She rushed to find the surviving baby and temporarily gave him to be fostered by Zhen Hui and Yue Yan, two responsible young ladies who lived in another section of the welfare centre.

They could not be sure, but it was not unknown for big disabled teenage boys in other welfare centres who were sleeping in the same room as the babies to have misjudged their own strength as they tried to quieten a crying baby – resulting in a baby's death. The team immediately separated the sleeping spaces of girls and boys, and younger and older children, despite their limited space.

Throughout 2006, an average of eight abandoned children each month were admitted to the welfare centre. Most were babies who would previously have had little chance of survival. From then on, whenever a new baby arrived, Kyla gave it to Zhen Hui and Yue Yan to provide temporary safety. This continued for a short time until Kyla brought them a sixth baby. It was then that they recognized a specific need. Kyla worked on the ground with the welfare centre and David worked on the board to provide both space and funding for the first official baby room in the Spring Project.

ICC recruited and trained extra caregivers to provide day and night cover but in doing so greatly raised the expectations of what the job required. There were new regular routines of washing and feeding children, changing nappies, and keeping to the structure and rules implemented by ICC. Those who had come in from government departments were used to the "iron rice-bowl" system of lax supervision. They were never expected to play with the children. Those who were content with sitting by, idly reading newspapers and ignoring the needs around them, began to struggle. All but two of the original staff members quit the project.

The remaining carers had a heart for the children and quickly adapted into the new system. The Spring Project hired their first two local staff members, Yao Ling as Kyla's assistant, and Yang Cai Ling as the project's accountant. They then moved to hiring young rural women and gave them basic training on how to care for children with disabilities. As time went on the staff became family – caring for the children was no longer a job. They were not there to get paid but because they loved their charges. Kyla recalls, "They began to make things at home, to bring in presents, to take the children outside or even to their homes. They began to love work – coming in on their day off because they did not want to be away."

Gradually the welfare centre allowed them to increase their footprint. The baby room was in the main four-storey building. They were next given several tiny terraced village houses, each not much more than two rooms, which were located a little way from the welfare centre compound. The roofs were falling in, the floors were covered in glass and rotting wood, and the electrics were just plain dangerous. Graham Young, by now an ICC board member as well as International Director of MMM, again returned to China with a team to work their renovation magic on the derelict buildings.

In six weeks, MMM gave ICC four purpose-built homes for different groups of children. Each had a living room and TV, two bedrooms, a toilet and a kitchen/utility room. The electricity supply was installed to high Australian standards. MMM, this talented organization made up of a variety of tradesmen, lived out their vision, as Graham said, "of using the skills of Christian builders to provide a space for God to transform lives".

In October 2006, all of the girls moved out of the damp, cold ruin, where water flowed through the middle of the courtyard, into the four-roomed houses. Each acted as a separate group home for three to four girls of similar ages. Some of the houses were still occupied by welfare centre staff and as they moved into new government housing, ICC added a further home. The final house that was vacated was that of a family who had fostered several children on behalf of ICC.

The team were amazed to see how almost all of the children began to sleep soundly when divided into smaller groups of the same gender with round-the-clock care that they could trust. This had a huge impact on their energy levels, which increased as their stress levels decreased. Despite their disabilities, they were more able to engage in daily activities because they felt safe.

Karen Norman only noticed the changes when she came back from her annual break. "They were dramatic; like the difference between the behaviour of the girls and the boys during the period the girls' home was open and before the boys' accommodation was upgraded. The girls were clean and began to take pride in themselves, while the boys did not have that motivation."

Alison Kennedy and Janet Sagan, a Canadian-Chinese physiotherapist, began to teach ICC's local caregivers some basic therapy techniques so that the children would have fuller lives. Activities and circle times were set up for the children. The residential carers who worked with the girls in decorating their new homes saw the pride each girl had in having her own bed, in her own room with just a few other girls. Judy Elliott, on returning from the UK, said, "It was as if the carers had become like children – it was touching to see grown women enjoying themselves. They were also learning how to play."

They stopped cutting the girls' hair short and dressed them in pretty clothes donated by the local Chinese community. The girls loved it when short-term team volunteers put ribbons in their hair or painted their nails, telling them they were beautiful. Slowly, the girls started to believe it for themselves.

Soon after ICC had taken over the courtyard, Helen Harris visited from Hong Kong.

This little boy grabbed me and would not let go. He was holding hands and hugging me, all the time with a huge smile. He wouldn't let me out of his sight all day. For a year after that I often thought of him, wondering what had happened to him and how to sponsor him. My daughter Chloe visited Hengyang a year later and found him. 'He' was actually a beautiful little girl, eight-year-old Yang Hua, but at the time her hair was cut very short and the boys and girls were dressed the same. I returned a month later and recognized her immediately. Since then we have visited her every year. She has a beautiful disposition, but the condition she has makes it very difficult for her to retain memories. We have sponsored her for over a decade.

ICC believes that it is not just involved with giving the children a higher quality of life but also with a child's future independence. This means dealing with the holistic needs of children with disabilities. The project required a dedicated therapy department so, in October 2007, Alison Kennedy chose two of the caregiving staff who demonstrated patience and willingness to engage the children individually, and began to train them on the job. That team had risen to nine professionals by early 2017, comprising mainly locally trained therapists.

One group of young men with cerebral palsy could not sit up and become involved in activities without specialized seating. The therapy team were creative and, just as Lyndel had done in Changsha years earlier, Alison arranged a local carpenter to build them wooden chairs. Li Bin, Xin Yuan, and Zhong Peng were then able to sit comfortably and engage in a group circle time. That provided a springboard for them to start learning in special education programs, which led to them developing computer skills. These boys are now independently mobile, using specialized wheelchairs provided by donors.

Their lives, and those of others, have been greatly impacted by the therapy support. It has helped them eat safely and engage with the world. Other improvements included bathrooms that were modified with new equipment to allow the children to shower more easily and to develop greater confidence toward their independence.

By mid-2007, some of the children were developing well but were unable to go to a mainstream school because of their disabilities. ICC then began its first special education class for school-age children with learning potential. Yang Lao Shi (Teacher Yang) was initially a caregiver who was promoted to teach a small group of children. She was devoted and loving and allowed the children to flourish. Her classes grew as more children were added to the education program.

Zheng Ming was the first to show a real aptitude for learning and soon surpassed the other children, so ICC applied for him to attend the local school. In Hengyang, as in Changsha, ICC faced opposition but now had the experience to prevail, which gave Ming the opportunity to get the higher level of education that she needed.

Hannah Chih, a volunteer from Taiwan, had been recruited by David to work with ICC in Changsha for several years before moving to Hengyang. Hannah's passion for young people led to the establishment in 2006, as mentioned earlier, of a simple craft workshop for those who were over eighteen years old. The room was crowded and was far from ideal but it laid the foundations for a dedicated workshop later on.

The young people loved the opportunities to work and talk during the craft times. Sheng Qi had been at the welfare centre since he was seven and was frightened of the foreign team when they first came to Hengyang. In the workshop he found that he could bead and make jewellery, helping to grow his confidence and dissolve his fears. As Hannah spent more time with him, he began to discover his value.

The team noticed that the welfare centre staff would gravitate away from children with Down's syndrome, a genetic condition associated with intellectual delays. When the ICC team first came to Hengyang, babies with the syndrome rarely survived, as it is both difficult and time consuming to feed and care for a baby with the condition. One month in 2011, when ICC's project was full to overflowing, five babies and toddlers with the condition were abandoned into the welfare centre and before ICC got to hear about it, four out of the five children had died.

The fifth child was a tiny emaciated critically ill baby girl called Jade. When the ICC team found her, she had chest and skin infections, which they treated, as well as giving her a nasal feeding tube. The team knew that they had a big educational task before them. Earlier in the year, Karen had taken a child with Down's syndrome to see a doctor. The doctor took a brief look and said, "She's going to die soon."

"Why?"

"She's got Down's syndrome."

"But you don't die from Down's!"

The team fed and cared for Jade on ICC's baby floor and she slowly began to gain strength. She grew from baby to toddler, full of joy, and showed great potential. A year earlier, a baby with Down's syndrome, called Ping, had been adopted overseas and the welfare centre agreed to submit Jade's paperwork to the Beijing Centre for Adoption Affairs.

She was matched with a family almost immediately and a few weeks before she left she stole the show by dancing at ICC's twentieth anniversary celebrations. Hengyang government officials and ICC's team watched with smiles from ear to ear as she sang, danced, and charmed the whole room. When the welfare centre staff saw how much her adopted family adored her, they began to advocate on behalf of children with Down's syndrome.

Karen was responsible for much of the medical side, establishing a clinic in March 2007, something she had never done before. She felt out of her depth, as they were on call 24/7. At midnight they might be told that a child had a fever. "How high is the fever?" The carer would put a hand on a child's head and say, "Oh, 38.4." Karen would pick the thermometer up from the desk beside them and say, "Please use this to take the temperature and tell me what it is."

There was little concept of basic medical care in early 2007. "Take the temperature and remove the ten layers of clothing from the child, give them lots of water, and keep them clean." These experiences allowed the caregivers to learn how to help children survive a short fever.

After a year, they made contact with the Swinfen Trust in the UK, which provides access to free specialist medical advice in the developing world or war-torn areas. Karen could go online in the evening with the details of the child's ailment and the test results, and have a response overnight from senior medical specialists from around the world who freely gave their time. This was a resource Karen couldn't even access in Australia. It supplemented her own knowledge, allowing her to go to the hospital with a diagnosis and a plan for further testing and treatment. The telemedics could connect them with leading specialists within China who in several cases were able to save children's lives.

One malnourished little girl from the welfare centre called He had been abandoned because she had a huge tumour on her back. The hospital said that she was going to die. Karen fought for a biopsy and the tumour turned out not to be cancerous. The telemedics suggested a medication. "We watched while the tumour shrank to the point where you could barely feel it under her skin." That little girl was soon adopted.

Qiu Jing had an extremely complex heart condition; in fact, several of his organs were on the wrong side of his body. The Swinfen telemedic consultations resulted in him being admitted to the Shanghai Children's Hospital for two major surgeries. The doctors did extensive testing but then called Kyla to say that his condition was probably too complicated to operate, and he may not survive.

They recommended against surgery but had enough confidence in ICC to let them make the final decision. Kyla called the telemedics, who consulted their pool of specialists familiar with the procedure and the skills of the surgeons in Shanghai, who recommended going ahead. ICC raised funds for the surgery through several churches in Australia.

Jing's complex operation was a success and he was soon matched for adoption with a family in the US. His treatment was published in telemedic articles as a case study and he became a poster child for the American paediatric cardiac department where he received follow-up treatment. He was the first of many ICC children who had cutting-edge operations in Shanghai or Beijing.

Karen spent a great deal of time at the local hospital and her kind, generous, and open nature meant that she developed a deep relationship of trust with them. The head of the children's department was especially supportive and encouraged his staff to learn and gain confidence. A different attitude toward children with disabilities was developing.

Many of the older children who had been forced to provide for themselves simply to survive had deep mental scars that could take years to heal. They had to learn how to be children again, and trust that adults would take care of them. With girls and boys separated, routine feeding schedules in place, a safe place to sleep, medical treatment from the simple to the complex, and caregivers they could trust, the children began to transform into what they always should have been – little kids.

On one of her earliest visits to Hengyang, Judy Elliott was crammed into the big boys' room during a tropical downpour. "There were twenty-five foreigners and forty-five kids in this room just five metres square. We had the music on, games out, and chaos reigned. I sat next to this shy, undemanding seven-year-old boy. In the middle of all of this noise, he played jigsaws with me for two and a half hours. He was so easily entertained because of one person's love and attention."

Ten years later, that little boy, Wang Zhi Hong, received his first pay cheque for managing a shop in the lobby of the new five-storey purpose built Spring Project Children's Care Centre run by ICC. Judy Elliott comments, "He was the inspiration for me to realize why I had travelled all the way to Hengyang and do what I did. There is so much need – we see it on the TV all the time – and then change channels. It's very satisfying to know that you *can* make a difference for someone so far away."

CHAPTER 18

New Growth

The retired colonel looked around as his guests arrived. Nearing sixty, he had the bearing and manners of a senior military officer. His sharp and intelligent face sported a tidy moustache not often seen in revolutionary China. He was not tall but as the visitors entered the room they straightened up and saluted him properly. "*Ni Hao*, Colonel. We are very pleased to meet you." The colonel looked surprised.

The guests had all served in the Chinese army, many in junior ranks, and were now officers of the Changsha Welfare Centre. Their host was Colonel Hang Khee Tan, former Chief of Armour for the Singapore army. They clicked immediately, sharing their military misadventures.

Hang Khee's background was of immediate interest. "What could a former senior army officer be doing in Changsha?" They gave the colonel great respect – he could communicate with machine-gun fluency in several Chinese dialects, albeit with a Singaporean accent. It mattered not that he was retired, from another country's army, and now, puzzlingly, was the newly appointed China Operations Director for ICC.

The ICC board offered him the role of China Director on the back of his experience and enormous energy. David had appreciated Hang Khee's heart to follow God and to accept the strong call to the nation of China, but not the advantage that his military background would have in strengthening the authorities' confidence in ICC. "He was able to do a unique job of turning the frosty relationship with the government into the strongest position we had ever experienced."

This military connection was critical to Hang Khee's success in developing high-level relationships, or *guanxi* (关系) with the authorities. The head of the security bureau had merely been a lieutenant colonel in the artillery, and, despite having been in a different army, rankings were still respected. In time, Hang Khee became genuine friends with many of these senior figures in Changsha. He was a *zhan you* (战友); a "war friend"; a comrade in arms – and remains so today.

ICC's new China Operations Director had retired from the military in 1998 to serve with a Chinese-speaking church in Sabah. He had bumped into a colleague from the Singapore navy on a speaking visit to the Singapore Military Christian Fellowship who knew ICC board member Terry Phillips, who in turn introduced him to David.

Hang Khee's first comments were, "What would I do in an orphanage? I'm an army guy!"

But his wife Victoria said, "Maybe you should look at it."

"No way!" was his firm response.

However, as he explored the opportunity, he found David impressively clear about the mission of ICC and was captured by the vision. Hang Khee said, "Victoria is very good at this patient waiting. She always says that if God opens a door it is right to go through it. I am a man of action. I usually look to batter it down – and if it opens it's the right thing to do!"

So it was that in mid-2007 Hang Khee found himself being proudly introduced to Changsha by the head of the local security bureau. This connection soon bore fruit. A dispute erupted after it transpired that the landlord of the apartment block where ICC was renting a couple of staff flats had been illegally tapping electricity. The authorities sent four inspectors from the electrical company demanding immediate recompense – from the tenant if necessary. When Hang Khee appeared they recognized him and his military connection and they happily shared that they had seen action in Vietnam fighting for the Chinese army. The problem evaporated. "Go home, friend; we'll resolve this."

Hang Khee's arrival in 2007 coincided with new challenges facing ICC as China's economic boom created double-digit inflation. The renminbi currency was buying a lot less as it appreciated, driving up local costs at a time when much of ICC's income was in foreign currencies. The large team of locally employed, ICC-trained carers – critical for looking after the children – were being tempted away to work in factories. Their families often pressured them, saying that working with children with disabilities was too menial. Factory work could pay two or three times the wage of a carer.

The ICC budget was now close to US$1 million a year. David and Richard Harris, the board chairman, felt keenly that ICC had to develop to grow. David says, "We needed to equip ourselves to provide the care and support that was needed. Little children have complex needs but we had proved that we could help them flourish. We could not stop caring for these children as they grew up. As time went on, caring for young teens with disabilities would be a different task."

A great deal of effort and energy had been invested in developing the projects in China but there was much more needed to develop a critical mass. The first decision taken by the board was to pay David a salary. "I had raised my own support from the very beginning and God had provided. A group of people and one or two churches had donated my living costs and I was thankful for their consistent love, support, and confidence."

The board now tasked him with the overall fundraising of ICC. "In some ways I felt more responsibility as my faith in God's support now had to cover the whole work, rather than just my needs." But David and Linda were also expecting their first child, so he was grateful one extra burden had been lifted.

David had first inspired people outside China on his fundraising tours to Australia, Canada and the UK. Then as executive director, and now as founder of ICC, he made a powerful impression speaking in front of churches, company meetings, and individuals.

Kirsten Britcher noted: "It's part of his charisma; he has no guile. He knows how to work a room but he is accessible, believable, and genuine... And when he asks you to get involved – he is irresistible."

David did not just mobilize strangers to go to China; he mobilized the person who led his youth group back in the UK. After her husband died, Jean Mclellan could not understand why God had said to her, "You will reap a worldwide harvest." Yet, through David and ICC, He opened a door to the world for Jean later in life. "I have since ministered in China, Hong Kong, Singapore, Taiwan, South, West and North Africa, and Canada."

Within China, Hang Khee, right from the start, had to meet the challenges by strategizing, setting objectives, getting things done, working to a budget, and executing policy. This was easy for him – he had been doing this for the army his entire career. Transferring his management experience to the NGO world was not. In the army, orders were given, understood, and immediately carried out. The volunteer culture however did not take kindly to receiving orders. "Managing an NGO is totally different. I had to start again. For instance, most of the staff were ladies, and I was a gung-ho soldier!"

Volunteers had to learn to interpret Hang Khee's emails, which often used acronyms or abbreviations and left them mystified. On the other hand, the volunteers were experts in the fields of occupational or physical therapy, or nursing.

Hang Khee laughed. "I didn't know the difference between OT and PT."

David's view from the beginning was that once you're in the ICC family, you stay in the family. ICC's core belief is that every life has value and every child deserves to live their life to the full – with meaningful activities and relationships. So he had been developing a vision for children to be cared for in small, family-style group homes, rather than institutional centres. The board agreed that now was the time for family units to become a key element within all of ICC's projects.

Group homes, gathering children of the same sex and similar age and ability, would provide the closest thing to a family that ICC could offer those young people with intellectual disabilities who could not study, work, or live independently in the community. They would also provide a model for the long-term care of young adults to the local authorities.

One of Hang Khee's first challenges was to manage the family-style apartments ICC had purchased. Two were in the Changsha suburb of Sen Yu Jia Yuen and two were in Wan Shi Jia. The flats were divided into the group homes with rooms identified to specific occupants who now lived in family units.

Most critically, Hang Khee managed to secure the title deeds to the properties in the name of ICC in order to confirm ownership of the assets. This was important in China where the legal ownership of assets was not always clear. One challenge was that from time to time NGOs were not permitted to have a bank account in China. Hang Khee always managed to preserve ICC's account and keep it separate from that of the welfare centre. ICC had always kept strictly accurate accounts at project level to be transparently accountable to donors and the authorities.

The Lighthouse and Canaan Homes

In October 2007 Hang Khee was introduced to a landlord who was interested in selling an old three-storey factory building in the south of Changsha, in an area of the city called Xin Kai Pu. The international board happened to be in the city at the time – and as they walked on broken glass, gazing at the bare concrete columns of the ruin, a new vision took place.

If this place could be bought, it could house the majority of the children from the rented accommodation in one place. The squat three-storey building took up the whole side of an open square but it was otherwise surrounded by high-rise residential buildings that hummed with activity day and night. The location would give the children a sense of living among ordinary people, while showing to the community the human side of what they saw as broken children.

After heavy negotiations, Hang Khee settled at a price of two million yuan but the Chinese economy was hot and the price kept going up. What turned the deal was that a local Changsha lady connected with ICC went to the seller and burst into tears in front of him. "Look at the children! What will happen to them?"

Hang Khee phoned Richard Harris in Hong Kong on Christmas Eve, knowing that anything can be done there right up to the very last minute. He needed a for-profit company in Hong Kong to be set up, which was the only kind of company that could own the building under Chinese law. The company, Lifeline Services, was hurriedly established and ICC purchased the property for 2.3 million yuan (US $250,000). Hang Khee said that year: "It was the best present I could have had."

It took an astonishingly speedy nine months and a million yuan to turn a ruin into a modern children's care home. When the Lighthouse opened in September 2008, it even included a lift – a first in a country where lifts were only employed in buildings over four storeys, even in disability centres. Dr Liu, ICC's Changsha project leader, moved thirty-six children from their rented flats into their brightly painted new home, organized into family units. The board official opening and the fifteenth anniversary of ICC took place in October 2008. Hang Khee proudly presided over the ceremony like the proud father of a newborn.

That the home was up and running in record time was due to the project management skills of Justin, whose lively personality and professional construction skills persuaded, cajoled, and laughed contractors into doing more for less and twice as fast. This big, tall Aussie, occasionally seen with multi-coloured hair, was a great favourite, not only among ICC's children, but also within the Changsha community. He periodically appeared on Hunan Television talking in the local dialect about disability causes. Justin had the honour of being asked to carry the Olympic Torch through Changsha for the Paralympic Games in 2008 because he was so respected as a foreigner who had come to China with his family to look after Chinese children with disabilities.

Justin and Lisa Anemaat were standout volunteers for ICC, despite the demands of their own growing family. Lisa gave birth to her first child, Tyson, in Changsha at a time when foreign births were almost unknown. They served in the field for fourteen years in significant leadership roles. Lisa became the Team Life Coordinator and Justin stepped in at a critical moment to serve as the Changsha Project Director. They came to China as a couple and left with four children.

Hang Khee's attention was next extended to those children ICC could teach to lead independent lives in the community. He kept saying, "Where do they go when they grow up?" Some of the children were now in their mid-teens and unless they were very high dependency, they needed to go to school and to work. In China, everyone is expected to work; there is no unemployment/ disability support.

Just alongside the Lighthouse were a series of garages – basically open concrete shop spaces at street level. A few of Hang Khee's contacts in Singapore chipped in with some money and purchased two of the garages, one for boys and one for girls. Justin renovated them into self-contained dwellings, with a kitchen, toilet, living space, and bedroom providing accommodation for those over sixteen who could live independently in a sheltered environment close to assistance. They called the garages the Canaan Homes (家 南, *Jia Nan*), and the independent group living concept was born.

At all the projects, ICC has established home schools with teachers who draw up an individual education plan to develop each child's independence, work, and recreation goals – teachers like Hannah Chih, who set up the art and craft workshop in Hengyang. Dianne Hall later came to help with new creative ideas and projects for the teens to work on.

This resonated with another project close to Hang Khee's heart, a Vocational Training Centre (VTC), whose purpose was to expand education, training, and ultimately work for young adults outside the residential homes. Even for children too disabled to be truly productive, it provided a discipline where young adults would make cards, thread beads, or construct packages for the post office. A local businessman, Mr Zhen, provided the premises. When asked why he did this for no return, he said coyly, "To get a good name for my business."

Hang Khee was philosophic about his time with ICC. "I learned something about myself – and it changed me a little. I decided to take time off almost every weekend to go to the flat at Sen Yu to play with children. Me, an old soldier on my knees! The adults there would ask me why I did it – it became an easy way to show God's grace!"

CHAPTER 19

Support for the Family

David and Linda had planned to start a family a year after they were married in 2002. As that year had turned to four years, the waiting and desire for a family increased, and so Jamie's birth in December 2006 was a time of great joy.

"After all the years of holding, caring for, and loving ICC's children, I was delighted to hold this long anticipated baby boy in my arms. Linda and I were ecstatic with the adventure of being new parents. I'd changed many nappies over the years, burped numerous babies, cleared up the milk that they threw up, and changed their clothes. Holding my own son in my arms reminded me of each of those moments afresh."

David and Linda both loved the name Jamie, and Linda felt strongly about his middle name. She had been deeply touched by the story of Simeon, an elderly man described in Luke 2:25–26 who had been given a promise that he would not die before he saw the Messiah. When Mary and Joseph brought their new baby to the temple to be blessed, Simeon finally gazed on Jesus; he knew that he could now depart in peace. "It was our wish that our first son Jamie would have that same desire for Jesus as Simeon had – so he was named Jamie Simeon Gotts."

Kieran Caleb Gotts was so eager to enter the world in October 2008 that he slipped out into the hands of the midwife while the doctor ran toward them down the corridor. Kieran is an Irish name and ironically means dark one – even though he was pale with strawberry-blond hair. Caleb was someone who would trust God no matter what giants he faced in his life. "Many years ago, God had spoken about how I was someone with the same kind of spirit as Caleb in the Old Testament.[16] We wanted Kieran to have that same spirit."

Home life for Linda and David now felt complete, although David still wondered if the adoption of a less fortunate child might be in their future. It was a good time for ICC as the care for the children in the ICC projects continued to mature, even though each day brought new challenges. One of these challenges was the knowledge that, across the welfare centre compound, more children were being admitted – and they simply couldn't help them all.

China had come a long way in its care for abandoned children but many were still abandoned and many were still dying of neglect. Although the flow of healthy baby girls had eased because they could be adopted overseas, that prospect didn't yet exist for children with disabilities. Without sufficient resources to care for them, they would certainly perish.

David had always struggled with how families could abandon children with disabilities. "Although I was filled with a deep compassion for the children, I found it hard to extend any compassion to the parents." He would hold a frail and malnourished newborn in his arms, look into their perfect face, and find anger welling up inside him. "How could a mother carry a baby inside her for nine months only to abandon it at night in a bus station? I was so overwhelmed by what I was experiencing that it left me little capacity to understand what had led parents to that point."

One night, as Linda was feeding Kieran, she noticed his hand would sometimes twitch. She told David, "Quick, look now!" As David reached out to his tiny son, just three months old, his hand gave a tiny, jerky movement. Linda picked Kieran up and passed him to David, when suddenly Kieran's body went limp. David had experienced special needs children in China having a seizure and so he called the medical helpline for advice.

He was shocked when, instead of the expected reassurance, the nurse told him to take Kieran immediately to the emergency room. The concern in the voice of the nurse rang in his mind as he held Kieran on the way to Vancouver Children's Hospital. Before they knew it, their tiny baby was hooked up to several beeping machines.

The next few days were a blur as Kieran was seen by emergency physicians and admitted for more tests. Kieran's seizures continued and so did the tests. An MRI was ordered to try and understand the cause. They stood by their sleeping boy's bed as Kieran's neurologist, Dr Linda Huh, gently shared that they had found a rare neurological malformation called polymicrogyria in Kieran's brain, which would cause seizures.

David and Linda were shocked. The doctor's explanation was lost as they tried to take in what she was saying. What did this mean? "A million questions came about his future independence and mobility. Would he be able to drive a car? Would he go to university? We stayed strong through the conversation but wept when we were alone."

David and Linda walked through weeks of uncertainty as Kieran's seizures would subside and resurface. Medications were changed to find the right one, but each took time to work. Days were filled with apprehension as they watched the clock, counting the length of each seizure, knowing that after five minutes Kieran would need to have rescue medications. "This was a painful and intense season in the life of our family. Not only were we contending with seizures that could strike at any moment, but we also were coming to terms with the fact that Kieran's whole life, and ours, would be altered by his neurological condition."

David had spent much of the previous twenty years caring for children with disabilities in China but Kieran's diagnosis had brought David and Linda first-hand into the great pressures on those families in China. They too had gone through the joy of the birth and like them they realized that a child with a disability or illness would be life changing.

The difference was that the parents of the children that ICC serves in China had minimal assistance. They faced a lonely and isolated journey. "We were grateful never to feel alone and were surrounded by compassionate individuals, doctors, social workers and specialists with great expertise."

The Canadian government health service also covered the majority of the medical, educational, child development, counselling, and physical, occupational, speech, and language therapy costs. "I could not imagine how we could have coped without the support of our health team. We needed that support."

Few families in China have access to those kinds of specialists – and being rare such treatment is costly. David had met parents who had mortgaged their homes and borrowed as much as they could to help their child "only to find that the magic solutions they were offered didn't help their child at all".

For many families, it becomes too much to bear. "They don't know how to advocate for their child, and become more desperate and alone as they try to navigate a system that can't provide much help. These pressures cause many couples to split up and it is easy to see why children might be abandoned."

David's realization

David began to appreciate afresh the complexities that lay behind the decision to abandon a child. "I got it. I got why families buckle under the pressure of dealing with complex health issues. I began to have a strong empathy for those in China that were desperately looking for help for their child. ICC's plan to reach into communities and provide that support was not only important, it was vital."

The opportunity to sit down with parents who had made the decision to abandon their child rarely arose, as abandonment in China was illegal. Parents went to great lengths to ensure that their child could never be traced back to them. The one-child policy left grandparents worried about the continuation of their family line – something that only a male child could ensure.

David was now recalling his early days in China when he saw that grandparents might pressure their son into taking the child away after birth, often without telling the mother that she would never see her baby again. A daughter could mean potential financial insecurity for the child's parents. One day she would grow up and marry into her husband's family, leaving the parents without a child to support them in their old age.

> We occasionally began to meet families in the
> community who had a child with a disability. In
> the early days, children with a disability were rarely
> seen as they were shut away. Our hearts broke as we
> heard stories of desperation – of families trying to
> stay together, but simply not being able to cope with
> the immense stresses of being parents of a child with
> special needs. Tiny step by tiny step they slid toward
> hopelessness and the painful decision to abandon their
> child.

ICC had created an infrastructure that was delivering support services to the children under their care – and it was making a difference. They now had a loving family home structure and caregivers. Children also had access to medical care, special education, and physical and occupational therapy to help them reach their full physical and mental potential. Their journey toward the fullness of life was becoming a reality.

David thought, "What if ICC could reach out to families in the local community that had children with disabilities? What if ICC was able to become the support system for families that had a child with special needs so that they never had to make the painful decision to abandon their child?"

This was a different journey. David had gone from judging parents that might abandon their child to now wanting to pour the same kind of love into them as ICC did into those children within the project.

David shared the idea with the ICC team, relating that God was revealing a piece of ICC's work that up until this point they had not seen. It was as if they had been looking at just one side of a coin, but suddenly the coin had been flipped. On one side was ICC's care of abandoned children with disabilities while the other side was dealing with the root causes of abandonment by supporting families at risk. That way the child would stay with the family and the whole family would avoid the pain of abandonment.

The team was more practical. How could this be done when everyone was stretched to the limit? Would the government be willing to let ICC work outside of the welfare centre? How would it want to control ICC's work in the community? They didn't feel ready, but on one thing they were agreed: if there were a chance that this could happen, God would equip them.

The welfare centre director listened politely as David shared the community idea but he could tell from his face that he was concerned about the same issues as the team. "He felt that if parents learned about the work of ICC, it might lead to even more children being abandoned – as they would see that there was a place where they would receive great care. He didn't think that the support we could offer outside would be enough for families to stay together." David came away empty-handed. Perhaps the timing wasn't right.

ICC's children had practised dances and songs for weeks as the tenth anniversary of the opening of Oasis House was drawing near, and everyone was busy putting the final touches to the party. ICC had arrived in Changsha in 1994, opening Oasis House in the January of 1997. The journey had been one filled with many bumps along the way, but the team felt that the transformation that was evident in the lives of the children was something to be publicly celebrated.

ICC invited many senior government leaders to attend. Many of them had seen the children develop over the years – a testimony to how love, care, and support could transform a child's life and make them a valuable part of Chinese society.

The children sang and danced their hearts out as best they could, all dressed in beautiful new clothes. Children in wheelchairs sat next to those who were able to stand. Those unable to sing acted their way through the songs with almost coordinated waves and smiles and shining faces. "Just over ten years ago these very same children had been struggling to hold on to life itself."

The banquet after the celebration with all the government leaders, ICC staff, board members, and the children was held on a river ship that cruised along the banks of Changsha's Xiang River. It was freezing cold and the new Changsha Director for Civil Affairs was trapped with David in the small sheltered VIP area.

David knew that it was one of those moments. ICC had just demonstrated ten years of partnering and achievement and been given a seal of approval by Changsha's deputy mayor who had affirmed the work. Taking a deep breath, he again raised the idea that ICC could help to stem the tide of abandonment in the community rather than merely dealing with it once it had happened. David was impassioned. "How could we expect to see abandonment reduce if we didn't provide what families needed?"

Again the director and the vice-director listened politely to his arguments.

The director turned to his deputy with a look. He finally turned back to David and said, "Yes, we think the time is right. Let's begin to form a plan to help families in the community."

Sam Hills, a young woman from Australia, had wisdom beyond her years. People could see that she was a special person. She had graduated in occupational therapy before moving to China to work with ICC. Sam put her hand up to work on the other side of the coin and lead the Community Outreach Programme (COP).

Over the next few months, Sam worked tirelessly with the Changsha team putting the pieces into place so that they could reach out to families in need. A joint venture was signed with the Disabled People's Federation that would enable ICC to establish a community centre to which families could come for support. But Sam's vision was not only for the COP to be a centre to which families would come, but that she should also send her staff into family homes so that ICC could better understand the needs of those they were caring for.

Sam told of a case where a child with disabilities was abandoned by her parents into the care of grandparents. The grandparents were now elderly and the girl a teenager – and they could no longer physically carry her up the five flights of stairs to their apartment. The girl became shut away, never encountering the outside world, while the aging grandparents worried themselves sick about how to provide care for the girl when they were no longer around. It showed how necessary this work was as a part of ICC's delivery of services.

Sam, her staff, and those who followed her, reached out to hundreds of families providing them with the support to help them stay together. Families with special needs children began to come together in support groups and learn from each other. Children would be taught to walk by ICC therapists, others would receive education from ICC's teaching staff, and young people joined ICC's Sheltered Workshop, learning skills to contribute to the community. They were no longer isolated.

It was not lost on David and Linda how fortunate they were in being in Canada, whose system prioritized caring for those with special needs within their own family. Kieran began to thrive with the love and care of his family and the expertise of his team – just as those in ICC's Community Outreach Programme did too.

CHAPTER 20

The Spring Flows

The Spring Project in Hengyang, hidden from the public eye as so many welfare centres were, often suffered from frequent water shortages, electricity cuts and, in the early days, poor phone and internet access. In heavy rain or snow, the red soil turned the hilly roads into muddy rivers. The heat of summer would transform that same red soil into plumes of dust that every passing motorcycle or car would churn into a choking cloud, making the city centre hard to reach.

The winter of 2008 gripped the area with a snowstorm so extreme that the president of China came to visit Changsha. Every tree was encrusted with hardened snow, pipes froze the water supply, and power cables collapsed under the weight of the ice. The crisis that gripped the city hurt the Spring Project more, with no electricity and running water for eight days.

Communication with the outside world was cut as mobile phone batteries ran out. The cost of coal and candles soared as power lines collapsed. The bitter cold closed the roads, so members of the team walked 2 kilometres through the snow to commute to the orphanage from their homes, bringing with them as much food as they could carry. Children stayed in their beds under as many blankets as they could muster. Alison Kennedy went from room to room playing the guitar and singing songs to keep spirits up.

When the power was eventually reconnected they realized how closely the foreign and local team had worked together. It bonded them to work harder for the children against their common challenges and it was rewarded by the fact that all of the children had miraculously survived the winter. It seemed as though the weight of the work that Kyla and her team of international volunteers had been doing was now borne by everybody, making it easier to bear for all of them. They provided a support system for each other later on as they were periodically traumatized by the rawness of what they were witnessing. They cried together when children died, they remembered the promises God had given them, and they put in long hours each day to keep the project moving.

David and Kyla would speak often, discussing how to keep on strengthening and broadening the work that God had led them to establish. "My confidence grew as I saw them endure the cruel winter weather of 2008. So many other people would have given up when facing such challenging circumstances, but Kyla and her team relied upon God and each other and demonstrated that they could deal with each crisis that they faced."

They spoke of how they could build on the new "togetherness" and from this they forged an even stronger desire to truly empower the local staff to lead. Kyla's eye for people who could step up to more significant roles was sharp. She would invest in them as they grew into the people she knew they could be. There was lots to do, including developing more sophisticated care techniques and work policies, recruiting and training staff, managing the renovations of new buildings, developing medical, therapy and education departments, preparing sponsorship reports for donors, and negotiating with the government for more resources within the welfare centre.

Judy Elliott thought Kyla was inspirational at this time. "She had a great ability to allow people the freedom to be themselves. She empowered people because she trusted God was doing something in them. It was a huge gift because it gave people value. She was a listener who valued us Western visitors who just popped in. That made us feel that we counted and built a powerful team spirit."

Medical support

Before the ICC team arrived in Hengyang, the children received very little medical· care. Indeed an analysis showed that all of the fifty-five children were diagnosed with a different disability, illness, or special need. The two nurses, Karen Norman and Kyla, found that while they could give their medical opinions, they often had to fight for the necessary surgery.

They spent time researching local doctors, finding hospitals that would perform surgeries, and trying to raise the money. They began to send children for surgery to hospitals in Changsha for clubfoot, cleft lip and palate repairs, and as far away as Shanghai or Beijing for more complex procedures such as cancer treatment and heart surgery.

David remembers a phase of weekly calls when "Kyla would tell me of another abandoned child that desperately needed lifesaving surgery. This could cost upwards of US$5,000 – often much more – not a small sum in ICC's whole annual budget."

Just as David thought that ICC had reached a place of relative financial stability, a new request would come in, but they believed that each child was created in the image of God and filled with potential. Often the surgery would do more than treat; it was a healing such that the child could be adopted. "How could we say no to funding a child's surgery? We didn't know where the money would come from, but we trusted that God's heart for each child was such that He would provide. And He always did."

ICC also pushed for children to be immunized against common childhood diseases. The project was still just beginning in 2006 when a newly abandoned child arrived with measles.

The new team operating in a new place attempted to quarantine the child with little success, for not enough children had been immunized and the disease infected the whole community.

They continued to fight for children to receive prompt hospital treatment and were helped over the next year by a number of professional welfare centre staff that had been trained in more modern techniques within China's social welfare system. They began to replace the old ex-army cadres, and the awareness of the special needs of the children and the benefits of directed surgery increased.

Shortly after the ICC moved to Hengyang in 2006, a beautiful newborn baby boy was abandoned and admitted into the Hengyang Welfare Centre with a congenital stomach defect. This condition required immediate surgery after birth to ensure survival before blood poisoning set in. The ICC team decided that he would be the first disabled baby they would request the welfare centre send for surgery. The centre had a basic clinic but children with special needs were rarely admitted to hospital.

After some negotiation, the welfare centre agreed, provided ICC found the money for the required treatment. At this time, the city had limited resources for the high cost of surgery, so ICC budgets that would normally cover running costs of the project for a month or more were now spent on unexpected surgeries. The overwhelming medical spending for the babies, albeit still low by Western standards, brought ICC's China budget into crisis on a number of occasions.

For that first little boy they were too late; he died from complications from the surgery – a hard blow for the ICC team who had invested so much in him emotionally. Karen Norman, a nurse from Australia who had been serving in Changsha with ICC for three years before moving to Hengyang, immediately established a clinic for the early diagnosis of babies and children as they came in. Serious cases could then be quickly referred to hospital.

Though they did not know it at the time the welfare centre had taken notice of the way the team had fought so hard for the first little boy. As a result, when another sick infant was admitted into the welfare centre a few months later, it was their staff that remembered ICC's previous commitment. It was the first time that they had suggested hospitalization in Changsha – and Kyla jumped at the opportunity.

"By good fortune, it was a few days before Christmas, and we had already booked bus tickets to spend Christmas with our ICC colleagues in Changsha. We wrapped him up in endless layers of clothing and took him with us on the bumpy bus [ride for] three hours to the city." The little boy's surgery was successful and the team celebrated their joint success with a meal with the welfare centre staff. The celebration was repeated a few months later when a Canadian "forever family" adopted him as a permanent member of their own family.

By the time the next baby with the same condition was admitted, the welfare centre immediately sent her to hospital under the "Tomorrow Plan". This was a central government Ministry of Civil Affairs programme by which Chinese orphans were funded to have necessary surgery. The plan thankfully eased the demand for surgical financing from ICC.

This little girl blossomed after she was welcomed back from hospital for post-operative care and she was soon adopted by a new "forever family" in America. Her mother, Erin Schmidt, became involved in ICC's adoption advocacy campaign in the US to find families for ICC children who have been approved and have adoption paperwork and are waiting for prospective parents to choose them. The progression of support for children who require medical treatment to adoption has been one of the most significant changes over the years of the Hengyang project.

During this time, the survival rate of children rose rapidly but the team faced constant challenges as they tried to find more beds and the space to put them. Karen employed and trained caregivers to monitor the health of each child, from checking immunization records to regularly weighing them, and making sure they were taking the correct prescribed medication.

When ICC arrived, babies with surgical needs would die without any access to treatment. Now the government had a system in place to provide surgery. The welfare centre even began to suggest surgeries for the children.

The ambition of the ICC team was to model its key value – that each single life is important – in a low-profile, non-threatening way. Kyla, Alison and Karen spent a good deal of time developing personal relationships and partnerships with the government and other organizations. They wanted to provide an example of how their Chinese partners could advocate for their children to receive adequate medical attention.

The team also demonstrated what appropriate end-of-life care looked like, as some abandoned children were too ill to be saved. Those who died now did so in the arms of a volunteer or caregiver, rather than alone in a crowded crib. Kyla said, "We began to host small memorial services to commemorate those who had died in an effort to model our core value – 'the sanctity of life'. We invited caregivers to say goodbye and some accepted the invitation and permission to grieve." In a place where death was still frequent and children's bodies were disposed of quickly and silently, this was a revolutionary concept that spoke loudly.

As the mortality rate dropped, the numbers of children ICC cared for increased dramatically. They began with fifty-five children in April 2006; by the July of that year they had seventy-seven, and within a year there were over 100. They were constantly running out of space for new admissions. After securing a place for their first baby room following a long process of negotiation with the welfare centre, they soon filled it and required another room. Some of the new babies were already sleeping two to a cot.

The pain of not being able to help

In November 2007, eighteen months after starting the project, ICC could no longer manage caring for all the children who were pouring in. The constant influx of children never allowed the project to achieve stability and if they were not careful it would not be long before the cribs would be as packed with babies as they had been in the original welfare centre years before.

David Gotts and the board realized that 2008, the year of the global financial crisis, might be a bad year for fundraising and expansion, so they made the prudent but difficult decision to cap the number of children in the ICC Spring Project at 135.

> Kyla and the team wanted passionately to keep the door open to newly abandoned children. It was a devastatingly difficult decision to make but we knew that eventually the welfare centre would have to accept that they too needed to improve. We figured out how much space we needed for each child and informed the welfare centre that we could no longer take more children until more space was made available...

It was heartbreaking for the Hengyang team to see the newly abandoned babies and children going next door into the government welfare centre building where the mortality rate was still so high. They were so stretched, however, that there were concerns that the quality of care would regress if they had to cram more children into such a small space.

David travelled to Hengyang and secured two more floors of an old building and two derelict village houses from the government. They were at least able to send longer-term international volunteers and the short-term teams into the welfare centre every three months to assist with feeding, running snack programmes, and activities.

ICC could only take new children when the ones they had were adopted or passed away. It was like the early days in Changsha where they felt as though they held in their hands the power over who lived and who died. Kyla tried to balance the intake of children, selecting them by how much ICC could do for them, regardless of disability. "It was always difficult walking through the welfare centre with the goal of choosing a child. I was acutely aware that I would change the life of this child, while leaving other children behind."

On one occasion two spaces opened up. "We brought in a little boy with one leg, who we knew would be quickly adopted, and the other was a baby girl with severe cerebral palsy who had trouble feeding and would likely stay at the orphanage for the rest of her life."

A spot opened up following an adoption and the team prayed over a list of eight children. That afternoon, Kyla walked into one of the rooms in the welfare centre and a boy with cerebral palsy immediately stood out. She came back and said, "Jian is on my heart. What do you think about him?" A teammate said: "If we don't take him, he won't make it through the winter." Within weeks, he had put on weight and his cute, round face beamed at everyone. He quickly learned to speak and interact with the caregivers and the other children.

"We chose him because it was clear to us that God said: 'Pick him'. Then we had another miracle," said Kyla. "We discovered his intellect was fine, and in fact he was very clever." They put him in a conductive education class with other children with cerebral palsy but he quickly outgrew the group and was placed in a higher class. "Each time we chose a child, we were pained knowing that we were turning more away, but when we trusted that God was the one to pick them, it was easier to move forwards and concentrate our efforts on the children in our care."

Barbara's calling

One of ICC's earliest recruits for local leadership was Barbara Li Huan who had become Alison Kennedy's translator when she came to practise her English with the foreigners who had settled at the Hengyang Welfare Centre in 2006. She was having trouble at home, for her Chinese parents did not approve of her accepting a job from a group of foreigners who were looking after sick children when she was, after all, a talented young English language student.

Barbara deflected the pressure a little by telling her parents: "It's the only job that I can find so close to home. I'll do it for just a year, then I will have the experience to find something else." Barbara was passionate about the children, eager to learn therapy and education skills, and quickly accepted new concepts.

Kyla recognized that local, educated and talented Chinese staff who understood ICC's value system were always going to be needed to manage the project and advocate for change within their own culture and community. Delegation of responsibility to local staff, as they were trained, appointed, and promoted, was vital in building future leadership. The longer she worked in China, the more Kyla saw limitations in not having a native understanding of language, culture, routines, and how to address people with different levels of authority.

Barbara was appointed the Hengyang local project manager and moved to work in the education department, quickly becoming an important part of ICC's operations.

David recognized that Barbara had a natural talent – the perfect combination of a heart for the children and an ability to educate them. "Kyla shared with me the idea that we could truly empower Barbara to lead our special education in Hengyang. She asked if ICC would be willing to pay for Barbara to go to university in Sydney, Australia, to be trained in paediatric special education. We had never made that kind of investment in a local staff member before, but it was clear that if given the opportunity, Barbara would excel."

This was a great opportunity that her family approved of, and when she returned to Hengyang she took over the management of the education department, progressively expanding to include more children, training teachers, advocating for children to attend local schools, and finding resources for the ICC school.[17]

In 2007 ICC opened a kindergarten for all of the babies who had survived their infanthood and were now bright, funny, and rambunctious toddlers. They flourished there, learning through play and returning to their "family home" and caregivers each night. They loved and accepted one another, not noticing that some were missing eyes, legs, or had large scars from infant surgery. They laughed, cried, had appropriate tantrums, danced, learned to read and count, and celebrated birthdays, but most importantly became family to one another.

They were the first generation of children who had grown up without needing to focus on survival. They had food, love, care, cuddles, vaccinations, and medicine in a stimulating and safe environment. They had little experience of neglect and abuse, and were developing into happy normal children with disabilities. One by one, every member of the original baby room and kindergarten class has now been adopted, now living in a family of their own.

Adoptions brought a huge amount of joy for the ICC team, as some of the precious children they fought for were now going to belong forever to a loving family. Every adoption allowed ICC a place to give love, hope, and opportunity to one more child from the welfare centre. Still, it could be tinged with sadness as they said goodbye.

Healthy ICC babies became available for adoption from 2008 and were soon matched with forever families – but despite this the number of children with disabilities and special needs waiting for adoption continued to rise. In response to this, adopting families began to look more closely at children up to the age of fourteen with a range of special needs.[18] The adoption of children with more easily corrected conditions like cleft lip and palates, and conditions such as visual impairment, children in wheelchairs, Down's syndrome, or congenital heart disease increased.

ICC has now seen nearly 250 children adopted who live all over the world, with more than 100 children from Hengyang – and the numbers rise almost weekly. Few of these children would have survived without ICC's intervention, but they now have access to special education, medical treatment, and, most importantly, love from parents, siblings, grandparents, friends. A forever family provides a loving family support structure that beats anything an orphanage can provide.

Rich Hubbard remembered

Rich Hubbard was a globally recognized specialist in NGO work around the world and a much-loved founding chairman of ICC's international board, providing long time support and wisdom for David. He passed away in 2010 after a brave battle with an aggressive and rare cancer after being a role model to many. It was fitting that ICC's latest, most exciting project should be in Rich's memory. He had lived his life to the full, giving all of himself in advocating for the world's most vulnerable people.

David and Kyla had pushed the board from 2007 for all of ICC's children to begin living in family-style groups, following on from the group homes concept piloted in Changsha. David "knew that the cost of group home care was higher than having children in larger groups and that would have an impact on ICC's budget".

ICC had managed to keep to budget during the economic slowdown of 2008, thanks to difficult sacrifices by Kyla and her team, and God had continued to provide a growing income. "It was another moment when we had to decide whether money issues would prevail or whether faith in God's ability to provide would be our guiding light. As we prayed, we knew that we were being called to trust."

Their intention was that every ICC child would live in a home of no more than eight children, with the same caregivers setting a routine. The children would feel safe in their environment and build healthy emotional attachments.

The first three group homes were opened in a separate space in the Spring Project 2006 and added two more in the city itself in 2008. A group home for boys with cerebral palsy was created with a focus on providing conductive education and therapy with activities to improve their independence and quality of life.

The effect of group home care on the children's health, attachment, behaviour and progress was truly amazing – surprising all the staff, even those who had advocated for it. They saw children bond with their caregivers, and the staff developing a love for their children. Caregivers began to advocate for the children, noting when they needed medical care, more challenging activities at school, when they grew out of clothes, or when the babies were ready to eat solid food. The ICC team was able to take a step back; only intervening where needed. However, the lack of space meant that only a few groups of children could so far be set up in this ideal environment.

David and Kyla took note of successes and failures to prepare guidelines for family-style care in Hengyang. In May 2012, they moved their dream forward as sixteen children moved into two group homes in apartments in a new housing complex in the city. The Rich Hubbard Community Homes were opened by Rich's wife Lynda and their children Sam and Amy in a ceremony watched by welfare centre officials and ICC supporters who had come from all over the world.

Those who remembered the wild and unresponsive children who they had met when they first went to Hengyang now encountered a transformed group of young people, eager to welcome and show their guests around their new home. They now lived as a family of independent young people, helping their caregivers to shop and cook meals at home, and learning to trust and stand up for one other as brothers and sisters do. It was not only an important step in the lives of the children, but also challenged the perceptions of disability within the nearby community who saw disabled young people running errands and going to school.

Kyla is invited to design a new home

The biggest project was yet to come. It had taken the team ten years to get to the point where basic needs were provided for and children could trust that they would be fed, would sleep in their own bed, be warm, that they had a routine, and would be able to go to school.

In 2011, Kyla received an invitation from the Hengyang Welfare Centre to attend a meeting. They had a budget to build a new specialist multi-storey building for children and young adults with disabilities that would replace the disorder of the old buildings on the site.

The ICC team were delighted to see that the plans showed that the building could be made into family-style apartments, rather than the traditional, twenty-bed dormitories so often seen in welfare institutions. The success of ICC's Rich Hubbard Community Homes in the middle of Hengyang was already having a positive effect.

Though it was moving in the right direction, the plan still had a number of flaws. Bathrooms and kitchens were too small for wheelchairs and there were no elevators or spaces for therapy, teaching, and workshops. The most exciting thing, however, was that the welfare centre had shown the plans to the ICC team first to get their professional input at the early design stage and these snags could be corrected.

Alison Kennedy and Anna Jien worked extensively on the internal design issues, adding classrooms, therapy space, a clinic, and a separate palliative area to give critically ill children access to the highest quality end-of-life care. They followed the Rich Hubbard Community Homes model, where children were placed into a family unit with their own space, their own storage for their things, surrounded by their photos and those of their family unit.

The building was given its own Bible verse: "'The glory of this present house will be greater than the glory of the former house,' says the Lord Almighty. 'And in this place I will grant peace,' declares the Lord Almighty" (Haggai 2:9).

Work commenced in 2013 and the main structure was completed in 2014 ready to be decorated and fitted out with furniture. Kyla, Alison, Anna, and the entire team worked tirelessly to create a beautiful space filled with homes that were custom built to the children's needs. Children were divided by age and ability into groups of eight and it was planned that they would move into the new building group by group. For months, Kyla was asked, "When are we going to move into our new home?"

Finally the day arrived. On the morning of the official opening of the building and its accompanying playground on 11 May 2015, the kids were beyond excited. Little Cong Cong, despite her severe disability and limited verbal acuity, woke up at 5 a.m. with excitement and began yelling to wake everyone up. All the children and staff dressed in their new playground T-shirts, and spent the morning setting up the stage and trying to stop the hundreds of balloons from escaping from a big net that was holding them until celebrations began.

It rained throughout the night and into the morning but cleared up in time for the ceremony – with the local staff agreeing among themselves that they knew this would happen. As board members, old team members, and friends and donors of ICC arrived, the children's excitement grew.

And so did David's:

> The opening of the new ICC children's care centre in Hengyang was profoundly special for me. I looked out and saw Linda, Jamie, and Kieran sitting in the crowd. It was so lovely to have them with me in China to share this moment. I was especially moved because Kieran's neurological challenges were similar to those faced by some of the children now living in this new centre. They would have a loving home, amazing care, fantastic therapy facilities, great education, and medical treatment – closer to what Kieran would have in Canada. As at the opening of Oasis House, I witnessed that God was able to bring life in the desert.

David gave a speech, as did two members from the Civil Affairs Bureau, and the children put on a show with the teachers. Some danced perfectly, while others looked cute but overwhelmed as they performed in their chicken outfits, looking just like a regular primary school show. The visitors responded with huge applause, while teachers cried with pride for their precious chicks.

After the opening of the building came the real excitement – the opening of the new playground. Designed for children with disabilities by Rehabaid, a Hong Kong organization, with support from Alison and Anna, and donated by a family who adopted their daughter from Hengyang, it was a perfect addition. It has a wheelchair accessible swing, a quiet zone, and a noisy music zone to support children with sensory issues. The playground represents joy, and the children know that it has been designed and built especially for them.

Once again in the history of ICC, children were transforming before their eyes. The new building represented hope after suffering, a change from meaninglessness to wholeness, families for all of the children, and space to have meaningful lives – to play, to learn, to work. It also allowed ICC the opportunity to take in an additional twenty-six children, the largest addition to the project since 2007.

The Hengyang project is now home to 160 infants, children, and young people. Every Monday morning there is a free dancing session where music is broadcast into the courtyard and kids of all ages leap about. It is beautifully clean and does not smell. All very different from what David saw when he poked his head over a cot a quarter of a century ago.

Miracles in Hengyang

"There is no quick fix," says Kyla. "You can't jump in and out of a welfare centre and expect it to change." It takes a team – a lot of people – a long time.

The transformation in Hengyang is a result of eleven years of investment. Donors and child sponsors, international and local staff, long- and short-term volunteers, the board of directors, short-term team members, local government, and a huge community of people across the world praying, paying and visiting the project have all played their part.

Welfare professionals come from afar to see the Hengyang Spring Project and are inspired. The welfare centre has been encouraged to aim higher by following their example. What just nine years ago was a place of death for children with special needs is now a flourishing, beautiful home where every child has a family, and every child receives love, hope, and opportunity.

Buildings, however, are not the reason for ICC to be in China; rather it is the transformation of values about children. ICC sought to bring in a fundamental understanding of the value of life that could change the care for disabled children in a way that any amount of resources, funding, and equipment cannot.

Kyla says, "The team have celebrated victories: as they saw a local staff member take the time to brush the hair of a little girl and tell her she was beautiful, or bring a child to the clinic of their own accord to make sure he was given medication."

This transformation of values was illustrated one evening in December 2014, when during dinner, a beautiful six-year-old boy choked while eating his food. Though everyone tried to save him, he passed away.

As they had done in the early days of the project the team held a memorial and invited the staff. The whole project came and staff from the welfare centre management, office, therapy, and education departments grieved alongside his caregivers. The emotion was intense as the staff grieved at this tragedy, shedding tears and crying in a way that perhaps they had been unable to do before. Kyla shared, "I had to hold up his sobbing caregiver as she grieved the loss of this child – as she would the loss of her own."

The memorial "was full of grief, but at the same time beautiful" and included Bible verses, local Chinese songs, and a eulogy remembering his personality, his history, and his life in prayer. They continue to remember the little boy. His photo is on the wall, they share funny stories about him, they still cry together. Now, in the midst of this tragic situation, because children are cared for, because life is valued, God is glorified.

"Suddenly I realized. Only a few years ago, death happened here weekly and children's bodies would be put in a rice sack and carried out the door. No tears were shed, no prayers were prayed, and no one ever mentioned those children again."

CHAPTER 21

A New Day Dawns

Hang Khee's military contacts again proved valuable when David received an approach by a sponsor in Canada who wished to help to develop a welfare centre for children with disabilities in Henan Province in 2010.

He remembers receiving the warmest welcome. "Director Xue, of the Sanmenxia Welfare Centre, was a retired air defence major and gave me royal treatment every time I went." The good relationship smoothed the long process of approvals.

From the very first long-term partnership in Changsha, experience had shown that a strong cooperative relationship with the government was key to developing a successful project. David's hope that Oasis House could become a model of care that would be admired around the country was becoming a reality.

They found Sanmenxia to be a most liveable city. It was north enough to have government central heating when it was cold, and could use air conditioning when it was not – and unlike southern China, the air was dry. It was relatively small so you could walk everywhere. It had good transport and was not rushed or crowded, so there was time to enjoy the attractive parks full of flowers. It was still polluted but nothing like Changsha, where the mountains formed a bowl that trapped the coal dust.

Bruce Regier, a long-term China volunteer, was a fierce evangelist for the project and when the board agreed to go ahead, his family of five moved to Sanmenxia. Bruce established the project and developed a strong partnership with the welfare centre officials. When the news broke that he was leaving in 2011, Karen Norman had allowed herself the thought, "I wonder who they are going to ask to do that job? I know I wouldn't want to do it!" Almost on cue, ICC approached her to step up as the new head of ICC in Sanmenxia.

Karen

Karen was already an experienced China hand having lived in China for ten years, six years of which she was building the Hengyang Project with Kyla and Alison. By August 2012 she had blended her Chinese language, her knowledge of how to do business in China, and her experience of barefoot medicine with her professional experience to become the perfect candidate to lead the Sanmenxia project.

She was characteristically reluctant. "I was not excited. The idea was overwhelming and I didn't feel like I wanted to do it." Karen prayed about it, and when she did answer the call she was ready "God said, 'Perhaps you were called for a time such as this.'"

Breaking from the close, professional team in Hengyang was difficult but the transition was helped by Bruce and fellow Sanmenxia volunteers Janet and Daryl Conroy. Mei Koh, originally from Singapore but who served a long time in China with ICC, also joined her.

Karen immediately found the culture in Sanmenxia, which was 1,000 kilometres from Changsha, very different. It was much kinder and gentler than Hunan where everyone yelled at each other. "When you went to the market in Hengyang you felt angry all the time, always ready to put up a fight in case you were ripped off." In Sanmenxia they would say, "Let me discount that for you!"

On the other hand, you knew where you stood in Hunan – it was difficult to tell what the Henanese were thinking and they wouldn't want to offend you by saying something they thought you wouldn't like to hear.

The relationship with the local government was very cordial as ICC basked in Hang Khee's halo with the director of the welfare centre. David and the ICC board felt that Sanmenxia could provide a new model of managing children's homes. The booming Chinese welfare budget was leading to greatly improved standards for welfare buildings and the internal design.

David signed a management contract for an initial five-year period that required the government to pay for the building fabric (the hardware). The hardware was a vehicle to providing the quality of life for the eighty children. They called it the Sanmenxia New Day Disabled Children's Service Centre.

ICC's distinctive role was to invest into the software: to provide the staff and therapists, and train local staff in therapeutic techniques and basic medical and social care. ICC could demonstrate attitudes toward children's care including attention to detail, and the importance of adding respect and love into the mix that otherwise might not be considered. This would raise the quality of care not only for ICC children but also those in other orphanages.

The directors had a strong desire to improve their welfare centre and had progressively opened up to adopting ICC's management support, policies, and practices. However, there could still be difficulties in communication and values. As in Changsha and Hengyang, they had to upgrade the food, for the nutrition was inadequate, especially for babies. Karen had to keep plugging away to maintain standards by bargaining as in a market. She had to steer clear from gridlock, whereupon the director would be reminding her that it was *his* welfare centre and that he had the ultimate decision-making power.

As in the early days in Hengyang the staff were untrained – for them it was a job, not a family. The welfare centre thought that ICC wanted too high a staffing level, while ICC felt that they employed too few. At the beginning of the project, the norm was one caregiver for every seventeen children, but ICC had found that the optimal ratio for round-the-clock care in its orphanages was 1:5. Nevertheless, attitudes soon began to change such that even the head of the government's care department recognized that the carers had moved to thinking that it was not just a job but also a vocation.

Karen recognized that it was vital to preserve amicable cooperation and find a happy balance by understanding the different goals of the parties and by picking the right battles to fight. Her years of experience in dealing with Hengyang hospitals and her gentle, trustworthy character blended well with the welfare centre director's genuine desire for openness and improvement.

In a reflection of the new China, the director had earned his professional social welfare qualifications by passing the exams following an army career. In addition, he accepted Karen as part of the wider social welfare planning process. She was able to get some idea of the planning process that the local Civil Aid Department was undergoing and this helped her to understand the goals of the Sanmenxia Welfare Centre, including the thirty-year plan. She was then able to build ICC's planning around that background information.

After the first five years were completed the model was changed so that a single manager would lead-manage the original project with ICC continuing to provide the therapy. It also initiated family-style group homes, which ICC had pioneered in Changsha and Hengyang. This transitioned the older and more capable children out of the general welfare centre into separate units within the welfare centre with the aim of teaching them to cook, shop, and go to school independently, and eventually integrating them into the wider community.

China's attitude toward disabled people is changing. No longer are disabilities seen as a failure to be hidden away and blanked out. Welfare centres now look to the future – planning, not fighting fires. Future ICC plans include its Communities Outreach Programme in Changsha to help the welfare centre campaign for disablement issues and to support families in the community so that the burdens are not so high that parents with disabled children feel forced to abandon.

Medical treatment has also greatly improved in the last few years, with a much larger government budget. If anything there is often too much treatment, with children with colds being hospitalized and put on a drip. Surgery is often the first rather than the last option. Once in hospital, the doctors still take full control and ICC is not always able to participate in the child's care, as an individual, as it would in the West.

Sanmenxia has also developed standards for adoption, taking the ICC adoption process developed by ICC worker Angela Knapp for use in their other orphanages in Henan Province. The current rate of adoption is now fifteen to twenty children annually.

Through the local authorities, central government is encouraging local foster care to reduce the number of children in institutions. ICC plays its part in this as it knows the children and can select the best candidates for fostering.

When the deputy governor of Hunan Province (70 million inhabitants), Cai Zhen Hong, visited the Changsha project for National Disability Helping Day, he took pains to speak to the international volunteers about their daily lives and the challenges of the children. This exposure has provided much more attention to the plight of vulnerable people and helped the public to better understand and respect foreigners who have come to China to look after children with disabilities.

Part of David's charisma is that when he asks you to get involved he is hard to refuse. Hang Khee had agreed to do just two years in the difficult China director's role, but completed four. David felt Hang Khee's departure keenly, as he had all of the previous China directors. But God raised up another leader, Kyla Alexander, who not only had lengthy big project management experience in China but was also from the very heart of ICC.

CHAPTER 22

Changed Lives

Anna Jien arrived at the staff retreat in a Macau hotel, entered the elevator, and pressed her floor number. It was October 2009 and she was thinking back to when she was seventeen, when her heart was broken for underprivileged Chinese children after a family visit to China.

She had trained to be a paediatric occupational therapist and had been to China several times with the Canadian Christian Medical and Dental Society. Their medical team had treated hundreds of people waiting patiently in line in rural Ningxia Province. This whetted her appetite for long-term service and she quit her job at a hospital in Halifax, Nova Scotia, to concentrate on the search.

It took so long that she questioned whether indeed she should even become a missionary to China. Like so many others, she felt that God indicated that He would be happy with either decision. Finally, she had two interviews: one was for a prestigious job with a hospital in Toronto; the other with someone called Jannene Wall, to whom she had been referred by a David Gotts, who in turn had been recommended to her by yet another NGO. The hospital had lost Anna's papers so that interview was wasted – but with the ICC call, God had finally shown Anna His path.

As she mulled over her journey, the lift doors closed. Almost. At the last second, some fingertips, then a hand, appeared, stopping the doors from closing. The doors reacted with a start and opened. A tall blond-haired man bounced into the lift and jabbed at the "Doors close" button. "Hello," said the bouncy man, "you must be Anna!"

"Hello", said Anna, "and you must be David Gotts."

Anna arrived in Hengyang in January 2009 with the Spring Project in full swing. The team had a very good relationship with the welfare centre, who increasingly trusted the leadership of David, Kyla Alexander, Alison Kennedy, and Karen Norman in their work with disabled children. Liesel Luscombe, as a nursing assistant, added a great deal, not only with her technical skills but also with her introduction of consistency and discipline into the teenage boys' room – despite her pint-sized frame. Even though all Liesel's training had been with older people, she won the children over and they loved her. Hannah Chih had been involved with education with NGOs in China for over a decade.

The team had been strengthened by a couple from Brisbane, Australia, who had embarked on a new adventure in Hengyang in their mid-sixties. Ron Burns, a retired pharmacist, was an important addition as a mentor. The older boys especially enjoyed having a man around – even a cricket-mad Aussie. His wife Sue trained the caregivers by modelling care and play in the baby rooms. She also nursed several babies with suspected HIV in her own home, as they would cause great commotion in the welfare centre. Once stabilized, these babies were transferred to a specialist non-governmental organization.

Anna was comfortable in China, as she had attended her uncle's Mandarin-speaking church in Nova Scotia. It had been a good sign that when she wrote letters requesting funding support she received an outpouring of gifts from all over Canada – even from people she did not know. She found the best way to deal with things was just to accept that "This is China". The thick guttural Chinese dialect spoken in Hengyang was a struggle but, like David before her, she decided to fit in rather than fight.

China was very different for newcomers in 2009 than in the early days. They did not have to worry about food, or housing, or the cold, or being spied upon, in the way the early volunteers did. But it still wasn't easy. Without hardships to concentrate the mind, new volunteers would often come to China with high expectations of themselves and what they could give. It could take years to understand how China worked and it was easy to gather a mistaken perspective of China in the early days without the language and relationships. Volunteers would want to try out new ideas too soon and be disappointed when they didn't work. It was not that new ideas were not needed or accepted but it was easy to forget, surrounded by modern and sophisticated Chinese infrastructure, that one and a half generations was not enough to change centuries-old attitudes.

Anna found that she couldn't use many of her latest therapy techniques, which required twenty-four-hour support from the caring staff. It required training for the staff to fully appreciate what Anna was doing and that could take months if not years. In the early days, the carers would be happy if the children were merely fed and the rats were not nipping at their jackets. It was worse to apply new therapies that would be given up altogether after one or two attempts than not to try them at all.

Matters might come to a head when someone who had been in China for many years would say, "You can't do that!" The staff member, already feeling insecure in a new country might think, "What am I doing here?" Questions of identity and self-worth could arise. Occasionally an individual might come to China with an outstanding personal problem. The ICC recruitment process was designed to spot issues that could not be eased by simply running away from home, and which would be magnified in the field.

Anna took the attitude that she was not in China to work as a well-trained health professional but first and foremost as

Christian hands and feet, to help the children and staff as best she could. There was no other agenda. She knew that God wanted her to be in China for the long term – for three to five years at least.

Anna was instrumental in managing the opening of the Rich Hubbard Community Homes in Hengyang, preparing the young people for transition, and outlining a vision and mission for what the homes would represent. She got to know the children very well and had some favourites, especially Yang Heng Hua, who came to ICC when she was just days old.

Children of the group homes

Xu Lin had been abandoned because she had a rare genetic syndrome, which caused malformations of the skull and limbs, and possible developmental delay. Many people were startled when they saw the physical condition of the babies for the first time. Even Anna felt the same at first, but she knew that Lin's disability would make it hard to ensure that she was properly cared for, as feeding can be difficult.

In Lin's case, the doctors decided that she should have surgery to separate her fingers and toes, which were joined together. This was met with fierce resistance by the ICC staff because they were not confident that there would be any pre-operative investigation to determine the location of muscles or nerves between the bones. Bad scar tissue might prevent the very flexibility of movement they were seeking. This time, the welfare centre held firm against ICC's recommendations and Lin underwent the surgery.

Fortunately the surgeons missed cutting any vital nerves but the baby came back with insufficient dressings on the wounds and they had to keep vigil on the scars as they healed. The baby now faced a new life growing up in the welfare centre, but what was not widely known was that this lovely baby girl with a rare condition had been placed on an adoption list. It was highly unusual for a baby with this condition to be approved for adoption list, but by some miracle she was.

Soon after she recovered from the surgery Lin was matched with a forever family – and at the age of two she was adopted overseas. Anna met the family and knew that they were well prepared to care for Lin. She is now treasured by a loving family and has been given a second chance to have fullness of life.

Anna feels that "even in the severity of her birth condition and the foolishness of sending her for surgery, God had a plan for her. It showed that there is still love and hope in humanity. Although Lin's disability was difficult we loved her to bits. It illustrated to me a story of redemption."

Heng Zi has autistic spectrum disorder and could not bear any change of routine. "He freaked out when he saw food mixed together. He would drop to the floor and cry for half an hour." The carers figured this out and would carefully separate his greens from the egg and the tomatoes before he was given food. Anna began to help Zi regulate his emotions even though that was hard, as the room was noisy with big, boisterous boys with lots of energy who would yell, scream, and run around. Poor Zi would stand by the wall and not say a word.

He was bright, but often irritable – in the West medication would have been considered to help lower his stress but it was just not possible in China. It took time but Zi slowly began to communicate, even if his speech initially was an echo of what was being said to him. The breakthrough came when Zi began to sing, for children who have suffered terrible trauma often sing before they talk.

The team set him up with a strict daily schedule so that he always knew what to expect. His eating became calmer, with no tantrums. They discovered that he had a passion – art – and was happiest with drawing materials in hand. In his younger days at the welfare centre Zi was picked on by the bigger boys but as he grew older his response was to act as big brother in the Starfish Room in the new children's care centre, fetching lunch and dinner.

One of Zi's current duties is to mop the floor meticulously, as only an autistic boy would, starting at one end and finishing at the other, and pushing anything and everyone out of his way with a big smile. He highlighted yet another issue that had to be monitored now that the children were growing up. As he turned fifteen, the staff noticed that he would stand for hours outside the girls' area, hoping to catch a glimpse of one particular face.

Zi has thoroughly enjoyed his second chance in life but he was not able to have a third. He never made the adoption list in time and, being over the age of fourteen, the regulations said that he was too old. Yet he is still expected to develop into a functioning adult thanks to the help of one particular youth worker who has taken him under his wing. Anna mused, "He has taught me about the joy that he takes in the fullness of his new life. He has been transformed and is confident in himself."

Yang Heng Cong was a real favourite, arriving in ICC's care as a baby with severe quadriplegic cerebral palsy on 5 June 2006. She had big eyes and a bright intelligent face that just attracted people. She became one of the much-loved princesses on the first floor. About the only voluntary motion she could make was to smile. She was very shy and when she first met Anna she burst into tears. Over the years, the two became good friends. "She was very confident in her own skin," said Anna.

Both Anna and Alison provided therapy for her and felt she had one of the most tense bodies that they had ever encountered. It made swallowing and breathing very difficult. As she grew older, they were able to work on movements based on eye tracking and communication using her smile; a big one for yes, and a look down for no. As time went on she made noises – when she was pleased she purred like a cat; if she wanted attention she would grunt. With therapy she improved dramatically – developing into a sufficient communicator.

Cong Cong woke everyone up at 5 a.m. on the morning of the move by making loud noises of excitement. In early October, Anna went in to see her to tell her she was leaving Hengyang to get married. Cong Cong understood and burst into tears.

Just days after that, an unknown virus spread around the children, several of whom were hospitalized. Cong Cong picked up the virus too – but for her it was critical. Her tiny lungs could not cope and she passed away aged eleven, on 18 October 2015.

Anna grieved,"On the surface this was not a success story. Cong Cong would always have been dependent for the rest of her life. But to me she was a success. Her brief life brought the joy of life to others. There was something special about her that brought people closer to God."

When Kyla and her short-term team first met Ping Ping during a visit in November 2004 they found a tiny, frozen, unresponsive little girl. She had only recently come to the centre, and her tiny malnourished body had little hair growing on it. She made no eye contact at all. It was clear that she had been traumatized by her abandonment and by having to compete with so many others at the welfare centre. Kyla asked one of the team members to give her physical contact, and that person spent the next two weeks concentrating on her, holding her, and loving her every day. Minimal response came from the little girl, who hoarded toys in her hands but didn't play with them, and stored food in her cheeks like a hamster.

At the end of the two weeks, the team could only pray that Ping Ping had been given enough hope to survive. Three months later, they were overjoyed to see that she was still alive, albeit still apparently unresponsive. But after a while she walked over to the team for an embrace. Again, the team members continued the process of holding and loving her. They were rewarded just before they left by Ping Ping singing a little song – a wordless but joyful tune. She began to pull her visitor by the arm to indicate where she wanted to go. This process was noted. As the emotional team members said goodbye after their stay, one of the local government workers picked Ping up and held her, as if to say, "Don't worry. We know you love her. We've got her."

At the third visit, a staff member met Kyla with Ping in her arms, proudly showing that they and the older children had cared for her in the team's absence. They had figured out why Ping Ping's condition was improving.

In October 2006, when ICC had settled in Hengyang, Ping Ping was moved into the first girls' group home. She thrived within the less institutionalized group and started to attend kindergarten, but was unable to learn characters and mathematics as quickly as her peer group. It was suspected that her learning delays might have been linked to her traumatic history. Nevertheless, she coped well with practical work, played well with the other children, and became quite a chatterbox.

In 2012 Ping Ping moved from the welfare centre to the Rich Hubbard Community Homes in Hengyang with four of her "sisters". Under the guidance of the group home caregivers, she learned to shop at the local market, to clean, and to help her sisters with the washing. She is an amazing cook. In 2016 she started a vocational training program at the ICC centre, where she is learning new skills such as sewing and other handicrafts as well as some childcare skills. She has integrated well into the community and is still sponsored by the short-term team member who first held her frozen body during those two weeks back in 2004.

The Oasis House stories today

The pioneering children that David and the team selected for the first admissions into Oasis House are now in their late twenties and early thirties. Many have blossomed from ICC's little school to become independent members of the community with careers in the major cities of China. Some still live under ICC's roof but they are all examples of ICC children who have gone from near death to leading a truly fulfilling life.

Johnny Chen Shi is a graphic designer in Shenzhen and (of all things) a professional ukulele player. He is perfectly independent, using his wheelchair with great dexterity. He is a dedicated Christian and a frequent visitor to Hong Kong, where he supports ICC events.

Li Shi is Johnny's old flat mate in Changsha and is full of character, even though his spoken Chinese is so contorted that only David, Justin, or others who have spent time with him can understand his speech and have to act as interpreters. He moved quickly from ICC's school to a local school with admirable success. He now lives independently near the Changsha Lighthouse building where he can walk across and be a mentor and role model to the younger children.

Despite his almost unintelligible speech and cerebral palsy, he has two jobs. His unsteady gait means that he sways between the cars at traffic lights selling newspapers, rolling like a sailor; the drivers usually give him a little extra in recognition of his efforts. He also cleans offices – all of which raises money so he can fulfil his dream of training to become a church pastor. His ambition is to have a wife and family of his own.

Sun Wu earns her own living and is independent from ICC. She first helped the other children with their afternoon homework in the Lighthouse and was later trained to teach some special education classes. She worked for ICC administration who then encouraged her to move into teaching her own piano classes as her skills developed. More recently she accompanied professional Singaporean concert violinist Ning Kam in a public concert. There were few dry eyes in the house.

And very close to ICC's heart are the little boy Wang Gui and little girl Wang Hua, who kept each other alive in the same cot by their body warmth and friendship in the welfare centre even before Oasis House was conceived. ICC originally intended to take only boys into Oasis House but David knew that Wang Hua would die if she were to be separated from Wang Gui, so she was taken in as the first girl. She received therapy to help control her muscle movements, education, and all the special attention she deserved.

Wang Gui is very bright and has developed a deep interest in computers. After becoming an independent wheelchair user, he has now taken on the responsibility of maintaining computers not only in his group home at En Quan Yuan but also in the Lighthouse and the Vocational Training Centre in Changsha. In his group home he has access to nursing care, therapy, and small group activities for young people who have severe multiple disabilities in ICC. His physical challenges can involve long periods of hospital bed rest, lying on his stomach.

Wang Hua has grown from an affectionate girl with a sweet disposition into a talented woman with special responsibilities at her centre. She works in ICC's office, typing the personalized children's stories to update the children's overseas sponsors in the Hand-in-Hand programme. Every sponsor has an update about the child three times a year. The children love contact with sponsors and keep their letters close – and are even more delighted if their sponsor comes to see them. More recently, Wang Hua taught special education classes and spoke at a China fundraising event in front of 1,600 people.

Anna left Hengyang in 2015 to marry Chris Reeves after meeting him at Bethany, a retreat centre on Cheung Chau, an island in Hong Kong. It was the right time for her to go. As with all of ICC's long-term workers, those who leave are not forgotten. David repeats the familiar refrain at every farewell gathering:

"You can check out, but you can never leave the ICC family!"

Anna had a special six-and-a-half years watching Hengyang develop from a ruined four-sided house, a *siheyuan*, to the magnificent newly built five-storey Children's Care Centre Building. Still with a huge heart for ICC, Anna and Chris now serve short-term at ICC's Sanmenxia project.

Looking back Anna said, "I love Hengyang. If I had spent the rest of my life there, I would have felt my life complete."

CHAPTER 23

Building the House

Despite the bad year that was 2003, and the turmoil of ICC's abandoned and disabled children being forced out of Oasis House into six small flats, there were signs of new opportunities. The group homes concept was forming, the Lighthouse project was on the horizon, and ICC was being invited to explore the establishment of more projects in different parts of China. David and the board agreed that it seemed like the right time to expand.

Accordingly David and his team developed more sophisticated plans to raise more money for ICC and not only to support the projects. It was also time to build out the administration, accounting, and fundraising infrastructure. It is the lack of a developed business infrastructure that so often puts a limit on the work that an NGO can provide.

Not only did ICC need a strong team in China but it also needed committed support from those not in the field, many of whom, because of their role, could never be fully acknowledged. ICC needed those who could professionally manage the administration, organize the funding, and do the myriad of business jobs essential to a sustainable organization. Those who donated freely to ICC deserved an economical but professional administration team to properly account for and steward their resources. All of this information is given on the ICC website today at www.chinaconcern.org.

The administrative side of ICC was initiated in 1993 by Richard Hubbard,[20] David's earliest supporter and first employee. Richard put ICC, and the small town called Morpeth (where he lived in the far north east of England), on the map by freeing up David's time to concentrate on the work in China. He carried out the administration, computerized ICC, and drew up the early financial accounts for what little money came in. As time moved on, the board began to require budgets and balance sheets to implement a professionally accountable process – necessary if ICC was to extend its vision and ask for much larger support.

David regularly produced highly detailed business plans helped by Richard but this was very time-consuming, so the board approved the appointment of a human resources professional, Jannene Wall, to assist in his executive tasks. David could then spend his time ministering to people inside and outside ICC as founder.

Jannene had been a frequent short-term team member from as early as 1999 before David charmed her away from a successful career to a significant one with ICC. Her raw efficiency, constant availability, and out-of-hours hard work quickly made Jannene an indispensable part of the administration and it was not long before she stepped up to become Chief Operating Officer. David's vision matched Jannene's organizational skills in a very productive period for ICC. Her leadership skill led her into the position of Acting Chief Executive when David assumed his full-time founder role in 2015. Jannene completed this role in 2017 to be succeeded by Peter Maize, a highly experienced Asian NGO leader – and a local journalist of some note.

The executive administration has two broad business units: the China Operations and the International Operations. The Pastoral Care Team is, uniquely in ICC, regarded as a critical function, and also reports to the Chief Executive.

Kyla Alexander runs the field operation as China Operations

Director. She gives her leadership team great autonomy over their projects in Changsha, Hengyang, Sanmenxia, the Community Outreach Programme, and the finance and administration teams. As ICC operates like a sub-contractor in China, a relationship of partnership and mutual trust with the government is a vital factor for success and that trust continues through the organization.

Outside China, the International Operations comprises the Chief Executive, Head of Fundraising, Chief Financial Officer, and Head of Communications. David operates from Vancouver, with an office next to the ICC communications team and the Canadian National Office. Morpeth in the UK is still the centre for organizing child sponsorship, the Hand-in-Hand Programme.

The Chief Executive is located in Hong Kong, which is also a fundraising centre with handy access to China. ICC's global finance, talent, and accounting functions are co-located in Brisbane (which Jannene calls home). Rex Hills, a former business boss, came out of retirement in 2012 to become Chief Financial Officer and he upgraded still further the professional budgeting, cash flow, and accounting system.

As well as David and the Chief Executive, the board has extended the payment of salaries to certain key roles to facilitate the development of ICC globally. This payment is often for part-time roles, and staff are paid below the going rate – but ICC staff are driven by a Christ-like spirit of compassion. International volunteers working on the front-line in China continue to raise their own support from friends, families, and churches on their six-week annual holiday, although the board covers some expenses.

This unique global administrative structure works well because location is irrelevant compared to the availability and capability of dedicated and talented personnel. The communications or finance functions could easily be moved to Hong Kong if the right personnel were involved. Many people involved with ICC generously and willingly gift voluntary and low-paid time to ICC wherever they are around the world. This global administration network is effective and economical, made possible by the Internet, Skype, and frequent flyer miles. It would never have been designed like this from scratch but it works as a modern structure for modern times. ICC is a millennial organization.

The non-executive board of directors was established as David, even in his twenties, sensed limitations in his knowledge and experience. The mission field is littered with leaders who have failed or fallen by not being accountable. The board is the governing body of ICC and has the authority to challenge – and to dismiss – David if it deems it necessary. It provides a sounding board for ICC's executive decision-making.

The directors are balanced between business, pastoral, and health professional backgrounds, and include one or more former long-term China volunteers. They rotate on a three- to six-year basis. Directors bring with them work, wisdom, or wealth, but, most importantly, they come with a heart and a passion for children in China.

A big part of ICC's unusual structure is the national offices, which organize prayer and financing, and which are a source of talent for staffing ICC's operations regarding its "PRAY, GIVE, GO" mission statement. They emerged from twenty-five years of David talking about ICC around the world. Every now and then, an individual would be captivated to take on the role of spreading ICC's message of love, hope, and opportunity for abandoned and disabled children within their own country.

National offices meet donors, pray together, support team recruitment, distribute information to sponsors about their children, and organize the local Walk the Wall and the Circle of Hope dinners. They provide an opportunity for those at home who are called to become part of the passionate and committed global ICC family.

There are currently eight national offices – in Australia, Canada, China, Hong Kong, the Netherlands, Singapore, the UK and the US. They licence the ICC name and have a local board of directors, or "Friends of ICC". Directors are volunteers, and family members do not serve together to avoid conflicts of interest.

The expertise within the national offices has helped to develop ICC's high standards by contributing to professional policy manuals on topics like ICC's ethics, data confidentiality, personal conduct, organizational conduct, financial administration, donor policies, and child protection policies, as well as process manuals on emergency and crisis procedures.

Child protection policies have been drawn up with visitors to ICC projects requiring not only preregistration by the government but also references and background checks. The policies were introduced in around 2009, even though child protection had not been codified in China to the same degree by then. ICC has future-proofed its child protection policies by ensuring that they are at least as strict as the domestic laws and policies in countries such as Australia, Canada, and the UK.

Judy Elliott, who runs the UK national office and who was recruited by Richard Hubbard, said, "Lots of Christians think 'I can't leave home and my family to go to China but I still want to help where people are dying.' My short-term team was a wake-up call for me when I saw with my own eyes what I see on the news. It changes who you are. People who go on a China team come back long-term passionate advocates for mission."

Since the dark days of 2003, ICC has better understood its responsibilities to look after those who might suffer physical, spiritual, or emotional challenges as a result of being in the field. David was not aware until then of how to picture "worst-case scenarios"; he wasn't wired that way. His energy and enthusiasm had allowed him to start the work of ICC without too much thought. His youth, exuberance, and natural optimism pulled people along without regard to the consequences. As time went on, he had walked through situations where he had prayed for a better outcome and the worst had transpired.

The reality is that people can come to the field with life issues that may not have appeared important beforehand but in the stresses of the field can erupt anew. It may be family upbringing, relationships, or forgotten experiences that may drive new insecurities and fears. "Those issues don't disappear if you commit your life to moving overseas to serve disabled children." There is an additional level of stress when you live in a confusing and alien culture, and the supports and coping mechanisms that we lean on at home are absent. "The great intensity with which we work means it is inevitable that any issues we carry with us will come out," said David.

Living and working in China, serving orphans and holding dying babies can put you on a pedestal to your friends and family back home. "Supporters wave goodbye to their missionaries at the airport, sending them out to a difficult situation that can only be imagined." But if you are expected to behave as if you are on a pedestal, it's hard to share your difficulties. "When you are sending missionary friends out to serve in Africa or India, please recognize that they might be struggling with hard times. It's not just about the horror of holding babies as they die in your arms – your friend might also be struggling with issues related to their own childhood that they never dealt with."

As a Christian worker you're expected to be special because you have a close relationship with God. It was a shock to find that even Christians, trusted members of your group who had given their lives for disabled children in China, could betray, lie, steal, have issues with sexual impurity, keep important information from colleagues, be depressed, or walk away from their faith.

David shares, "We learned to live with more transparency and more accountability. If we had a concern about a situation, we didn't hold back as much as previously. We began to challenge things if they didn't look right and it would be a warning signal if the person took unseemly offence."

David's response was to implement a Member Care programme to cater for the psychological and spiritual needs of people on the field, and to see it as an essential cost of doing business. Such was the importance of Member Care that it reported directly to David as the founder. The first Director was Edith Watts, who operated from Canada with David. When Susanna Lynam took over the role was moved to China, with her husband Glen acting as the Hong Kong office's Administrator. Glen and Susanna sold their family home in Darwin to fund their early years in China.

It was critical to support people to avoid them slipping to a place where they could make devastating decisions. "People may fail in a way that will hurt them for the rest of their lives. We learned to try to support people through their China experience, whether they need it after one month or three years – or indeed after they have left ICC."

Prior to this, volunteers in the field were supported by an experienced field volunteer who served as a Team Life Coordinator (TLC). Lisa and Justin Anemaat pioneered this role in Changsha. They had already been in China with ICC for half a decade growing their own family, and had lived through ICC's experiences first-hand. As Justin moved into broader leadership responsibilities, Lisa continued to skilfully oversee the spiritual, mental, and emotional needs of the international volunteers.

Around the time that the board were crunching around the Lighthouse, ICC launched the first of its successful annual Walk the Wall fundraising programmes. This was a sponsored walk targeting 600 participants around the world to walk 10 kilometres – totalling the 6,00-kilometre length of the Great Wall of China.

The intention was to have Walks around the world on the same day, with Australia first in the time zone, followed by Hong

Kong, China, the UK, and completed by Canada some eighteen hours later.

There were two Chinese Walks, in Changsha and Hengyang, involving a posse of normally hidden-away children with disabilities being pushed in their wheelchairs by eager roommates. The authorities today will permit 1,000 people to walk for an ICC Walk the Wall, in a country where assemblies of even a few tens of people are highly restricted.

Walk the Wall has been a great success from the very first, when the money raised almost perfectly matched the 3 million yuan needed to buy and refit the Lighthouse. Few people thought the fundraising and the amount was a coincidence – more a case of God's accurate judgment.

The Walk is now held annually in the autumn, together with a springtime fundraising dinner, the Circle of Hope. Both are important fundraising events for ICC, and are held at about the same time in countries around the world.

David's vision for helping Chinese children with disabilities[21] to reach their potential to live as independently as possible is not complete. ICC is focused on creating strong families by encouraging the settlement of abandoned children in a family-style living environment.

ICC is now 25 years old and many of the children are now adults, but they still need the ICC family. The Group Home model has therefore become the model of choice rather than fostering with local families, which ICC attempted in the early days. It was found that the high levels of disability that were encountered meant that parents could only foster on a temporary basis.

Should ICC's role be a flicker of light in a lot of places, or a flame in one place? The work in China began as a spark, burst into flame, and has stayed lit even in the darkest of times. The next ten years will not just impact the children in its direct care, but will have a greater impact on the broader Hunan social welfare community and attitudes to children with disabilities across China.

The projects will increasingly be used to model therapy, medical care, and education for disabled children. The Community Outreach Programme – the first of its kind in China to provide practical support for parents within local communities – is an important part of that growth.

ICC began with the vision of providing love, hope, and opportunity to every abandoned and disabled child. David had no plan; he just relied on faith that God wants to do miracles. He developed the work step by step, dealing with each challenge as it occurred. ICC will continue in faith to – as the Chinese put it – "cross the river by feeling the stones".

CHAPTER 24

The Goodness of God

D avid and Linda's focus was to do all they could for Kieran. They were told that the seizures could be controlled through medication, and the doctors experimented with drugs and doses. It was incredibly stressful. Kieran could be anywhere and have a seizure. They were always on their guard, for Kieran could sometimes have twenty-four seizures a day. Infantile spasms such as these can damage the brain each time.

David and Linda were scared and found it hard to adapt to the new situation. Then in 2011 the doctors tried a new drug and the spasms stopped immediately. They were very grateful; they knew that the fewer the spasms before the age of three, the greater the likelihood that his development would be less impacted.

After Kieran's initial diagnosis family life settled into a new routine. David continued with ICC, and Linda was busy as a Missions Pastor at Tenth Avenue Alliance Church in Vancouver. Their routine was upset as seizures came and went, but they began to learn how to deal with Kieran's health challenges and life settled down. Jamie grew in leaps and bounds, and Kieran's development, though slowed by his neurological condition and the resulting epilepsy, was moving forward.

David reports, "In September of 2011, we were excited! Kieran was due to start day-care at Linda's church, the same one that Jamie had attended. Kieran would be playing amongst kids without disabilities yet get the support that he needed from

248

loving, caring staff. His first day got off to a flying start; he was beaming with pride as he sat on the stairs of the front porch – alongside his Fireman Sam backpack!"

A few weeks later, the three-year-old developed a nasty cough and had difficulty swallowing. His cute little lopsided smile had become frozen. At the children's hospital, he was diagnosed with pneumonia and his condition quickly deteriorated. The doctor thought that it might be a side effect from one of his epilepsy medications but Kieran's condition soon worsened and he was transferred to the paediatric intensive care unit.

The young doctor attending them was just about to move to the next patient when Linda asked him whether they had taken a second look at Kieran's most recent brain scan for any new clues. The doctor said, "Yes, you've asked us to do that… and we haven't yet done so."

He returned to share the news that Kieran's MRI scan had revealed a well-hidden mass close to the brain stem. It had been there since birth but had grown very slowly and even now was difficult to see. The shock was that the growth was unrelated to Kieran's neurological condition. The tumour was malignant and the cancer was inoperable.

"Linda and I sat down with Dr Caron Strahlendorf, the oncologist, and Suzanne Horn, his nurse clinician, and we felt crushed. He had already faced so many challenges, and here was something entirely new that could threaten his very life."

They sat and listened to Dr Caron as she outlined how Kieran would undergo a ten-month program of chemotherapy, along with a month of radiation. It would be a challenging year but she had a strong hope that Kieran's treatment would leave him cancer free. "We knew that Kieran's life was in God's hands."

Kieran celebrated his fourth birthday with his cancer behind him. It was a joy for the family, and the photos of Kieran eating birthday cake with bright blue icing filled their hearts. He had been unable to eat orally for a whole year and the best birthday present was not only for his cancer to be in remission but that he was now able to swallow and eat normally.

David's long-term credibility in China meant that he was able to share his personal story of dealing with a son's special needs with government leaders in China. "It was important to me that what I shared wasn't skewed toward the challenges and grief. We wanted the government to realize that our family life was full of joy. Despite the challenges, we could not imagine living without Kieran, who was and always would be a bright and shining light in our lives. We wanted to emphasize that we loved him just as strongly as our other son, Jamie."

The impact of Kieran's illness was felt beyond the Chinese government. Dawn Gage, who had known David since the very beginning of ICC's work in China, introduced him to the staff of Intech, a technology company in Shenzhen with whom she worked. Speaking in Mandarin, she explained that David was married and had two boys, one of whom was born with complex health issues.

She shared that David's life was now different because of his son. "It might look hard from the outside, but God is using Kieran and He has a special plan and a purpose for him." The Chinese love for children is powerful – and many in the room began to weep, including David and Dawn.

For nearly a quarter of a century, Dawn had seen David walk many paths filled with challenges – and learn many lessons. "It's as if each lesson was a piece of his heart that was cut out, but his heart kept growing back. I liken his situation to a Chinese proverb, 'Real gold doesn't fear the fire' (真金不怕火镰, *zhēn jīn bù pà huǒ liàn*)." Dawn doesn't know anyone who has gone through as much refining as David, yet he has continued to grow in humility and love.

ICC's board of directors, encouraged by their chairman Richard Harris, suggested that David should take a break in

2012. Chief Operating Officer Jannene Wall took over the Chief Executive responsibilities. David couldn't imagine having a sabbatical but he knew that his family needed his full attention and so gratefully accepted the offer. The rest of ICC's leadership team stepped up to take more responsibility.

Without the pressure of running an international organization David was free to focus his energy on his family. He also needed to recharge his batteries after the immense challenges of working in China. However, the relaxation of pressure also brought to the surface theological questions about the goodness of God that he had buried back in 2003. That was ICC's worst time – the year that David had to face betrayal by close friends, the loss of a project close to his heart, and a government ultimatum that may have closed ICC in China.

"My faith in God was so simple in the early days. God would speak and I would listen. He would ask me to do something, and I would do it. I trusted that God would make a way for it to happen."

Then he looked back and remembered many circumstances that he had faced where he had hoped and prayed for a different outcome, only to have to walk through the worst-case scenario. How could it be, even when you pray desperately for events to take a different course, that the consequences could still be worse than you had imagined?

These crises weakened David's assurance in the goodness of God. He had always lived by faith, and that meant retaining his self-confidence and a sense of security. "I had always carried the belief that things would work out in the end, but had now seen enough to know that it wasn't always the case. I now faced this crisis with Kieran in the ICU, struggling with pneumonia and a battle with brain cancer. I was no longer sure that God was good."

For the seven months that Kieran went through cancer treatment, David didn't know how to pray. It is much harder to keep faith if you can't say "God is good". He was wounded by all of his questions and the wound would not heal until he could devote a space to deal with it. And that space was difficult to find. "If your perspective of who God is and how He interacts with you isn't rooted in believing that He is good then how can you trust Him? Why would you want to trust Him?"

Yet even when David didn't know how to pray, he didn't feel alone. He still felt the love and presence of God. Nevertheless, he felt that a vast chasm existed between his questions and the place where he could truly return the love.

He stumbled through months of struggle and in May 2012 he attended a Christian conference on "The Dark Night of the Soul". David wasn't sure that he wanted to be there and didn't feel encouraged. All through the conference his heart felt disconnected as the words bounced off him. He had a strong feeling that the whole thing had been a waste of time, but on the last night the speaker asked if anyone would like prayer. David knew that many were praying for his family around the world so he raised his hand unexpectantly, thinking that there was little to lose.

"I sat there with my eyes closed and my hand raised. Someone gently placed their hand on my arm and began to pray. I recognized the voice as a lady called Nan, from my own church. The words she spoke were simple but they tore open my heart. She said: 'I just love the way that you hold Kieran.'"

David's thoughts played like a movie, and his pent-up buried hurts, emotions, and fears for Kieran's life burst forth. God was speaking directly to his heart. "David, you love Kieran so much. You carry him everywhere. You feed him and sustain him because that is what he needs from you. You protect him from harm, and are always aware of him. In the darkest times in your life, that is how I have carried you."

Right there and then, David knew a deep work was taking place in his soul. "My tears began to flow as the goodness of God became visible in situations where before I had only seen pain."

He could see that God had carried him through seemingly random, painful, messy, heart-breaking circumstances. "Something in my soul was set right that day," says David. "I knew, I knew, that God was good and He had been with me through it all. I may never understand why we walk through such difficult circumstances but I fundamentally now know that God is good."

David saw then that God protects when we need protection, He carries us when we fall, He feeds us when we can't feed ourselves, and He sustains us when we are dying inside. "It was transformational to know something so deep and to have such a powerful realization planted deep into my soul."

David returned afresh from his sabbatical to lead ICC in January 2013 and realized that although he had not spoken publicly about his faith questions, it had impacted his leadership. Now, the comfort of knowing that God was good meant that he could lean more on God for the wisdom, direction, and guidance that ICC needed. It had changed him in every sphere of his life – as a Christ-follower, husband, parent, and leader.

Toward the end of 2013, David sought a renewed vision for ICC by inviting all of ICC's staff, board members, advisors, and supporters around the world to engage in thirty days of prayer for inspiration. The process generated a flurry of exciting innovations and provoking thoughts from the team and supporters. "It was such a privilege to open the daily emails from people sharing insights about what they felt God was saying for the future of ICC. I read all the scriptures that they had read. I would hear the prayers they had prayed."

The messages resulted in ICC's future character being based on four principles: that they were to be a people of thanksgiving; a people who keep Jesus at the centre; a people of unity; and a people not afraid to embrace change.

David sensed God renewing ICC's work vision. It didn't cut across the past but looked to build upon the foundations of the preceding twenty years. China had changed dramatically, but it was clear that ICC still had a vital role to play in the lives of China's abandoned children – and in supporting the Chinese nation.

"At the heart was the desire to further develop the family-style group homes for abandoned children with disabilities that give each child the closest experience of family that they can have." That strategy also provided the highest level of services and support the children needed to flourish. The goal was to spread that model across China.

The strategy also meant strengthening the Community Outreach Programme that assisted families that had a child with a disability in their home, in order to minimize abandonment. ICC wanted to reach out to even more families in the community, providing the services that would keep them together, healthy, and happy.

The ICC community also felt that they needed to "give away" all they had learned over the years. If ICC could impart some of its hard-earned experience to others then the holistic model of care could become more widely accepted. "There are many across the nation of China, both Christian and those without the motivation of faith, who have a heart to help China on the journey of caring for children with disabilities."

Linda

Those who have met Linda Gotts are immediately struck by her elegant grace, good humour, and strength of character, as she too has walked through difficult times. "I know my wife is strong with a faith that leaves me amazed, and so we determined that we would live trusting in God who can heal – but also praying the prayer 'Thy will be done.'"

Not long after Kieran's cancer treatment had been completed, the family was delivered a further blow. Linda herself was diagnosed with breast cancer. David and Linda had worked as a team to support Kieran through his recovery and to ensure that Jamie was, as much as possible, able to live the life of a normal little boy.

"It was a shock to receive the diagnosis of Linda's cancer, and it felt like an even bigger challenge to see how I could provide normality for Jamie, help Kieran on his continued journey of recovery, support him in his development, and care for Linda as she faced chemotherapy and radiation. I also found myself living with so many questions."

What if he was left as a single parent? How could he cope on his own? How could they support Jamie through this? The circumstances were overwhelming but David knew that this time he was walking through this new crisis knowing that God was good and that made him stronger to face the future. He still didn't know the answers to the "what ifs?" but he knew God was carrying him, protecting him and sustaining him. He was no longer burying his hurt and pain, and could articulate his feelings to both God and his friends.

Linda faced surgery, chemotherapy and radiation with her characteristic fortitude until 2013. The family was able to settle and David returned to ICC. They felt gratitude and excitement, for they could now look forward and tackle the road ahead.

But their lives were not settled for long. In the October of 2015, the news came that Linda's cancer had returned. "We both cried at the news. Even Linda's oncologist admitted her shock. No one had expected this news. For me, the question 'what if' once again assailed me as the reality sank in."

It took a while for them to find their balance again, but they did, trusting in God. Once again their time was filled with medical appointments and treatment. Then, in October 2016, Kieran became increasingly unwell and his oncologist, and by now their friend, Dr Caron Strahlendorf, shared that tests showed his cancer to be not only incurable, but also aggressive.

Again David and Linda wept as Dr Caron said that the new tumour had been a side effect of the radiation treatment that Kieran had received five years earlier. David and Linda had known that radiation carried this risk but had taken the decision to proceed to give Kieran the best chance possible. They weren't ready to lose their little boy.

> Kieran underwent some mild radiation treatment to slow the growth of his brain tumour. All the way through, his sweet temperament remained. In fact, it seemed that he understood that time was now precious. He would sit on the sofa, and point to the seat right next to him to ask Linda to sit. He would lean in and enjoy the closeness of being together. Every night after dinner, he would walk over to me, climb onto my lap, and simply snuggle in. These precious moments burn deep into our memories.

On Good Friday 2017, David and Linda were able to reflect on the death and resurrection of Jesus as they went to Canuck Place, Vancouver's children's hospice. They had come for just a few days over the holiday to stabilize Kieran's health, with the family sharing a suite in the hospice just a few steps away. Instead, it became a five-week stay.

It was not made easier when on Easter Monday they heard that Dawn Gage, David's long-time friend and China field worker, had passed away at a relatively young age after her own lengthy and courageous battle with cancer. ICC would not have existed without Dawn, whom God had used directly in the chain of events that led to David standing outside the Nanning orphanage in 1992. She had devoted her life to the children of China and the interests of others, and would be missed by many.

We were so grateful to be together as a family in those final weeks with Kieran. Canuck Place offered us a place where he would get the best paediatric palliative care available. After the first two weeks, Kieran began to sleep more and more. Linda, Jamie, and I would spend time at his bedside, playing games, talking to him, and making sure that there was nothing left unsaid. We felt such overwhelming sadness. But there was never a day when we didn't feel the love and the goodness of God, nor find something within the day that brought us joy. We discovered that joy can even be found in the valley of the shadow of death.

Kieran peacefully passed into the presence of Jesus on 16 May 2017 at 5.05 a.m. as David and Linda held his hands.

Hundreds of people came together to honour Kieran at the service to celebrate his life. It reflected not only how much they had loved an eight-year-old boy but also how much he had impacted the lives of all those around him.

We are so grateful for the gift that Kieran was to our family. We were blessed to have this amazing boy with us for eight-and-a-half years. He helped us to experience a deep joy as he showed us what it meant to simply give and receive love.

The memories of his life are far stronger than anything cancer can take away. The knowledge of him being in the presence of Jesus, free from epilepsy and other health challenges, brings a smile to my face. We lost a son, and Jamie lost a brother, but we know that we will see him again. Until that time, the three of us will live life to the full – in his honour.

David's journey has taken him from a banking career in the UK at the age of nineteen, to live by faith in Hong Kong, Taiwan, and China, and to establish a mission for abandoned and disabled children. It has taken him from the poverty of the darkest of Dying Rooms in China's welfare centres to sitting with billionaires in their magnificent homes. And it has taken him into battle with his own faith over the illness of loved ones.

His journey was made possible because of God's unmerited favour – a grace that held on to him at times when he was no longer able to hold on. That grace has enabled him to have a faith that is strong and enduring, rooted in the goodness of God, and through it lives have been changed; not least his own.

"I am thankful that I am beginning to really understand how His kingdom comes. It comes in the moment when we reach out to those in need with love and compassion. His kingdom comes when we give ourselves over and over again and, as we are being emptied out, we find ourselves once more filled by Him."

David, Linda, and Jamie strive to keep a sense of normality as Linda continues her treatment. They are keenly aware of the goodness of God, and His call to pour out their love and lives to one another, to the children of China, and to the world around them.

"When we bring His love into a place of darkness and pain and choose to stay in that place, we do it because that's what Jesus would do. And His kingdom comes as we walk through challenges, trusting in Him and being drawn ever closer into relationship with Him."

CHAPTER 25

This is the New China

The journey from Hong Kong to Changsha can now be accomplished in relative comfort, by air or by bullet train. No longer does the train journey take twenty-six hours as David's first journey did, complete with blocked toilets and smoke-filled corridors. Passengers are whisked at over 300 kilometres per hour (nearly 200 miles per hour) directly from Hong Kong or Shenzhen to Hengyang or Changsha in not much more time than it takes to see a movie.

China of today – and yesterday – slides by at barely a tremble, with the pace only betrayed by the digital speedometer in the carriage. Outside the windows, tower blocks and black-belching industrial smokestacks merge seamlessly into farms and fields. One moment the scene is full of trucks, flyovers, and containers and, in the blink of an eye, steep, green-cloaked hills poke out of ruddy earth floodplains cut by rivers and bridges and dotted with cone-hatted farmers ploughing behind bullocks.

The trains are just one more miracle of modern China that has lifted many people from poverty to wealth in just over a generation. ICC's generation. The hardware is changing; the software – the hearts and minds – changes less quickly. When the bullet trains became common after 2010, travellers would stand in the corridors, afraid to sit in such luxury. Now, even first class is full, there is a McDonald's, a KFC, and a Starbucks at every station – and if you are lucky you might even get free Wi-Fi and a working escalator.

The new railway stations are cavernous, with the look and feel of an international airport. Hengyang station is designed to look like a Chinese temple – grand and imposing. Glass, marble, and steel are everywhere and so are the snags: buckets under dripping roofs and unintelligible announcements. This is China.

Things have moved so fast that in every glimpse there are vestiges of a life left behind. Black-windowed Porsches unload travellers next to older people bent double by a lifetime of carrying heavy loads. The overwhelming diversity in China pervades everything. Despite the outward appearance of success, many Chinese people work seven days a week, and struggle to get by.

People dress well but in a dated Mainland style. Girls dress five years younger than they should, in a flurry of non-matching colours and styles. Businessmen in sharp suits spoil the effect by wearing white socks and scuffed brown shoes with their pinstripes. Occasionally, someone cool will appear out of the crowd – straight out of a K-pop MTV set: buffed hair, necklace, black V-neck, and ear piercings that look like crosses. Popular and social media are rapidly influencing the attitudes of young people – so some of the software is changing, and changing fast.

China is undergoing a revolution in quality, but so far only first class and economy class exist. One can buy at a price either the very, very best from overseas or the just-good-enough local product. The handle on a mug may break almost immediately you leave the shop – but that is a result. The rest of the mug can still be used as intended. Reasonable quality at a fair price is only found in a developing society when the middle class has enough disposable income to demand it.

Twenty years after David's first short-term team arrived in Changsha, passengers will still find that Hunan is humid and muggy, polluted, drizzly and cloudy, often with mist to the ground. In late April, it is cool enough to need a jacket, even indoors with the air-conditioning. A wave of cigarette smoke explodes immediately the train doors open. Even a two-minute high-speed train stop is enough for a gasper on the platform.

The taste of coal dust hangs in the polluted air. On a bad day, inside a big hall or under bridges, it is possible to see dust and smoke swirling in the air. The mixture of exhaust fumes, cigarette smoke, and cooking oil at street level is almost asphyxiating, causing involuntary coughing as you walk the streets.

"Taxi muggers" fill the air with unbearable screeching to attract customers outside the station. They dodge as everyone pushes past. Queues for the regular taxis are long, showing the new wealth of the country. In the provincial cities, eight-lane highways link station or airport to the city, with dirt tracks leading off the route. Changsha has a Maglev train linking the modern airport with the new high-speed rail station.

These days, at least the traffic on each carriageway is mostly going the same way but occasionally a taxi or *san lun che* will still try to beat the jams by driving along the pavement or a short section of opposite carriageway. Cars will drive in the bicycle lane; motorbikes on the pavements; and vehicles will filter right and cut left to sneak across a straight road to avoid red lights. So much haste and yet often so little is accomplished.

China is safe for foreigners but the taxi driver still sits behind a cage separating the front from the rear seats. The traffic is terrifying, so you reach for the seatbelt – these days one is often fitted, but with no anchor point on the back seats. Even if the anchor is fitted, the driver may warn you not to use it for fear of leaving your clothes black, so rarely are they used. Sometimes he will take it as an insult to his driving that you want a seatbelt. So you say a silent prayer as the driver races down the highway to the first traffic jam in town.

Overhead at crossroads, large numerals count down to the green light to ease the patience of drivers. Bus stops show arrivals accurate to the minute based on an integrated GPS system. Confusingly, the use of GPS is officially illegal in China but every smartphone (and many people will have several) has an inbuilt location system.

The cash-only society has been transformed in just a few years to a highly sophisticated cashless economy. If you want to buy some apples from a street fruit stall you can do it through your mobile phone and the omnipresent WeChat app.

Old and new co-exist. A row of village houses now used as mechanics' garages sit next to a new glassy fifty-storey building with the hoarding advertising a global hotel group. The BMW showroom was built on a concrete platform in the middle of an isolated muddy field on the way to the airport nearly ten years ago. Now it is surrounded by flyovers and fast roads and has sprouted several new wings selling the latest models. Not far away is what seems to be the Mercedes Benz garage – although a closer look shows that it is a Chinese car showroom whose vehicles bear a striking resemblance to that famous brand.

The taxi weaves into the city centre overtaking scooters on the left and trucks on the right. China is even more the nation of shopkeepers than England, with every street level space occupied with commerce. Shoe shops sit next to motorbike repair shops. The next street has shops selling fruit and vegetables, mobile phones, *jiaozi* (Chinese dumplings), spectacles, jewellery, pharmaceutical products, mixed in with karaoke centres, a modern micro-supermarket, government or security buildings with fancy flashing automatic gates, phone card and newspaper kiosks, a bank here or insurance agent there. And everything is open until 9 p.m. at night.

As you come into town, the shops upgrade. In the last two to three years, much more has been spent on shop décor, and unknown Chinese brands have mushroomed, copycatting each other and Western brands. The best hotels have crept up from two stars to five but the taxi stops at the Jingjiang Inn – ICC budgets still stretch to two stars only.

The trip to the Changsha Welfare Centre is by another tiny taxi flagged down on a wet street. The inside of a modern Chinese welfare centre reflects the dramatic changes that have happened elsewhere in the country. They are clean and housed in modern purpose-built buildings. There are grab rails at hip level for the disabled and coloured cartoons on the walls. ICC's Changsha disabled children's service centre is so clean that you can eat off the floor. The children have modern play equipment: balls, toys, and lots of colour to assist interaction. Career caregivers keep the children cleaner, safer, and better looked after.

Hengyang was formerly a bumpy three-and-a-half hours' journey away, with one toilet stop, but now takes just thirty-five minutes on the train from Changsha. The old Hengyang Welfare Centre that could only be accessed by a steep muddy road is now minutes from the city by highway and a concrete access road, which keeps the mud at bay. The old buildings where ICC began have been bulldozed and have given way to a grassy platform. The government welfare centre built to the south of the compound has nine floors with lifts and disabled access. Most of this building is for the elderly, giving them a country view overlooking the valley below. The space released by this new welfare centre building has been turned into offices and staff accommodation.

The new multi-storey, purpose-built Hengyang Children's Care Centre for disabled children with disabilities is run by ICC. It stands proudly at the top of the hill with good views over the surrounding area. It boasts innovations like a central elevator and bigger doors and bathrooms for wheelchair use – all recommended by ICC. More robust materials that would survive the hard wear of a welfare centre were specified, initially at ICC's expense, until a donor came forward to cover it all – an answer to prayer.

The building is designed to encourage the group home concept with the children living in family units, where they can develop personal rather than institutional relationships. Each floor is carefully designated for a particular category of disability, with the most disabled on the lower floors, and education and therapy rooms on the upper floors. It boasts a clinic and an intensive care room for the very sick children.

The project in Hengyang is a benchmark for the care of disabled children in China, but ICC's efforts feel very much a work in progress. By showing how a few hundred children can be looked after, ICC has provided an example of how to care for the uncountable number of disabled children in China. ICC models how one life saved makes such a difference. The same number of children again that now live in the Hengyang Centre have been adopted, and this rotation continues. All of the adopted children have been brought back from near death to be able to live full, rewarding, and productive lives with their forever family.

China remains a country of huge contrasts. It is now a very wealthy country but much of the wealth is concentrated in a few hands. This means that there are enormous numbers of people still living in poverty, even though there has been a huge rise in average incomes over the last quarter of a century. The country can seem cold and austere at first yet it is not difficult to make hard, fast, and trusting friendships. In the streets one can see daily demonstrations of seemingly heartless acts but also the look of great joy on the faces of grandparents when they welcome their grandsons and granddaughters home from school. This exposes the inner heart of compassionate China. The Chinese people have a fundamental love for children – of both sexes.

China has extremely strict laws and policies for the protection of people with disabilities and yet inclusion of such people in schools, workplaces, and in the community is only just at the very beginning stage of acceptance. The country has improved a great deal in terms of facilities for the disabled. It is recognized that even low buildings need lifts for disabled people and ramps for wheelchairs. New welfare centres are purpose-built with design features that help carers and patients alike.

However, attitudes to disability take much longer to adapt: the hardware is easy, for that can be bought; the software in terms of the understanding of the mind takes generations longer to adapt. In the countryside, the old attitudes toward children, disablement and other signs of vulnerability remain firmly held.

Yet ICC has seen a dramatic change in the last ten years in the attitudes within the welfare sector toward disabled people. China is now the unassailable leader in the Paralympics Games, winning 107 gold medals in 2016, over two thirds more than the second most successful country, Great Britain. This, if anything, has touched the hearts of the poorer, harder-to-reach communities.

ICC has been very close to that change as it has happened, but it can also see where it wants to be – an integral part of helping China walk into its future with a system based on justice, inclusion, love, and professional care. The transformations in Changsha, Hengyang, and Sanmenxia are the result of nearly twenty-five years of commitment. ICC is continually evolving to stay at the forefront of caring for abandoned and disabled children. David's vision began as a series of entrepreneurial ideas inspired by his faith. The bringing of teams to China, the search for a permanent location, structuring of residential care, the group homes, community outreach programmes, the Lighthouse, and the Spring Project were all new concepts in their day. They were not perfect at first, but continued to evolve and inspire.

To see graphic designer Johnny Chen Shi in the street is to see an ordinary member of society – apart from his wheelchair. Despite his almost unintelligible speech, Li Shi, Chen Shi's old flatmate in Changsha, holds down two jobs and is looking forward to having a family of his own. Wang Gui and Wang Hua who kept each other alive by talking in their own language have jobs that suit their disabilities. Wang Zhi Hong runs a shop. Sun Wu has achieved grade 5 at the piano and has accompanied professional Singaporean concert violinist Ning Kam in a public concert. None of them would be here today if not for ICC.

David's vision is to have families convinced that their disabled child will get the support and care they need – as indeed Kieran did – and that the family will stay together. The ongoing work of ICC has meant that at least some abandoned children will wake up knowing they are loved and are able to live a life full of dignity. These are the things we believe will, can, and must become reality in China.

Water is stronger than stone. Laozi, the Chinese philosopher who lived 500 years before the birth of Christ, said that "whatever is fluid and soft and yielding will overcome what is rigid and hard". The people with the desire in their hearts to selflessly help others are that fluid. They may work unheralded, but they are adding to humanity day by day.

Epilogue

In late 2016, the *South China Morning Post* reported on a little boy who ran crying after his mother when he was abandoned outside an orphanage in Hengyang. The three-year-old was bundled out of a car with a bag of clothes and a note with his date of birth, but no name. He looked for her for some time and was lost in the streets before an old man took him sobbing and shivering to the police.

The journey that David began when he stepped through that Chinese gate at the Nanning Welfare Centre is not complete. It will never be finished – but perhaps we are at the end of the beginning. ICC has shown what can be done in China with the willingness of the government, and in a way that suits Chinese methods. Eventually all the funding will come from China. Eventually most adoptions will be by Chinese families within China. Eventually ICC's specialist work will be handed over to Chinese NGOs for good.

In the meantime, a small group of individuals who share a heart for abandoned children with disabilities have developed a platform to combine their professional skills and experience with local people. They have provided a source of pride for the provincial governments that run welfare centres in Nanning, Changsha, Hengyang, and Sanmenxia, successfully showcasing to the rest of China how to offer care for abandoned and disabled children.

ICC is a Christian development organization changing lives through bringing love, hope, and opportunity to China's abandoned and disabled children and young adults.

Alison Kennedy, who lives in Hengyang, feels that the theologian Jean Vanier aptly described what ICC is about – its people, and its work.

> To love someone is to show to them their beauty, their worth and their importance; it is to understand them, understand their cries and their body language; it is to rejoice in their presence, spend time in their company, and communicate with them. To love is to live a heart-to-heart relationship with another, giving to and receiving from each other.[22]

ICC asks its supporters for three particular things. To PRAY – to remember ICC and the particular challenges that its volunteers, carers, medical staff, and especially the children have to endure.

To GIVE – as it needs resources to help the children. The Chinese authorities are providing more and more hardware – the bricks and mortar. China is getting ready to take on the challenge but the country needs benchmarks and standards. ICC still has to pay for Chinese hands and feet to help. It runs very tight budgets but needs funds to look after the children.

Finally to GO – either to an ICC project or to a similar one to see how disabled children can be supported to live full and fruitful lives. You can help by going to see, or go to help, as His hands and feet. ICC would not have survived without people who were willing to dedicate from a few days to more than two decades of their lives toward the welfare of abandoned and disabled children.

David's challenge is to say, "What can you do? How can you help? Why are you so fortunate? Can you spread a little fortune?" Is it time for you to GO to China or somewhere else that is on your heart? You may never know quite how much influence you might have, or on whom. It takes so little to make a big difference in someone's life. You can see the hundreds of children who have been helped by the vision of one young man and his army of inspired supporters who chose to go and provide love, hope, and opportunity to China's abandoned and disabled.

You can follow what ICC is doing today on the website that accompanies this book (www.chinasoasis.com).

Endnotes

1. Or diapers.

2. Numbers 13:30–14:9.

3. See Numbers 13:32.

4. Nearly twenty-five years later, ICC's China teams still travel to China to encourage people with children on their heart to go and see the work and to continue the long-term vision. The impact on hundreds of team members, the children, the co-workers, and the Chinese government goes far beyond just a two-week mission trip.

5. Ross Paterson, *Heartcry for China*, Sovereign World, 1989.

6. These Dutch families still form the core of ICC's Dutch National Office.

7. Not his real name.

8. Gladys Aylward (1902–70) made her own way to China to help the Chinese people in 1932. Her tale is told in the book *The Small Woman* by Alan Burgess (1957) and slightly less accurately in the film *The Inn of the Sixth Happiness,* starring Ingrid Bergman (1958). She founded the Gladys Aylward Orphanage in Taiwan in 1958.

9. Since 1998 the Chinese welfare budget has expanded beyond all recognition. Its welfare spending rose from around US$48 billion in 2000 to around US$200 billion in 2016, or from about 4 per cent to 10 per cent of China's nominal expenditure budget (source: CNN, Port Shelter, World Bank).

10. Unlike today, there were still many girl children abandoned who did not have special needs.

11. Not his real name.

12. An organization that supports NGO work around the world.

13. John and Claire went on to found Eagles Mount Adventures, an organization providing underprivileged, orphaned, and abandoned children in China with special experiences through camps and outdoor activities.

14. Today, relatively few healthy babies are abandoned and if they are, they are quickly adopted. An overwhelming majority of abandoned babies have physical or mental disabilities.

15. Or bitterness.

16. See Chapter 2.

17. Barbara is still with ICC as a key member of the management at Hengyang.

18. China only allows adoption up to the age of fourteen to prevent people-trafficking, although the policy also prevents genuine adoptions past that age.

19. After which age a child can no longer be adopted.

20. Richard was not related to Rich Hubbard, the chairman from 2003 to 2008, who tragically passed away from illness in 2013. Richard was involved with ICC from the very earliest of days (see Chapter 2) as its first administrator, and served with ICC for twenty years.

21. This includes children and young adults that have been abandoned with health and medical issues. The word "children" is used to describe both children and young adults with disabilities.

22. Jean Vanier, *Seeing Beyond Depression*, Paulist Press, 2001, p. 19. Vanier, founder of L'Arche Community. He won the Templeton Prize in 2015.